1&2 SAMUEL
SURVIVING THE TENSIONS OF LIFE

JAMES C. DANT

Teaching Guide

SMYTH&HELWYS

Smyth & Helwys Publishing, Inc.
6316 Peake Road
Macon, Georgia 31210-3960
1-800-747-3016
©2002 by Smyth & Helwys Publishing
All rights reserved.

Library of Congress Cataloging-in-Publication Data

Dant, James C., 1961-
   1&2 Samuel : teaching guide / by James C. Dant.
   p. cm. (Annual Bible study)
   Includes bibliographical references.
   ISBN 978-1-57312-395-2
   1. Bible. O.T. Samuel--Study andteaching.
   I. Title: First and second Samuel.
   II. Title: 1 & 2 Samuel. III. Title. IV. Series.
   BS1325.55 .D36 2002
   222'.4'0071--dc21

2002014129

CONTENTS

Annual Bible Study

Cecil P. Staton, Jr.
President

David L. Cassady
Executive Vice President / Publisher

Lex Horton
Vice President, Editorial

Mark K. McElroy
Senior Editor

P. Keith Gammons
Editor

Kelley F. Land
Assistant Editor

Jean Trotter
Associate Editor

Jim Burt
Art Director

Barclay Burns
Vickie Frayne
Dave Jones
Graphic Design

Cover art
David. Andrea del Verocchio. 1470. Bronze. Museo Nazionale de Bargello. Florence, Italy.

1-800-747-3016 (USA)
1-800-568-1248 (Canada)

SMYTH & HELWYS
WWW.HELWYS.COM

Preface 5

1 & 2 Samuel for Adults

1 *Giving Attention to Tension* 7
2 *The Political Tension* 30
3 *The Theological Tension* 55
4 *The Relational Tension* 75
5 *The Spiritual Tension* 92

1 & 2 Samuel for Children

Teaching Children 109
1 *When I Am Afraid, God Answers Prayer* 110
2 *When I Am Afraid, I Remember God Is Strong* 116
3 *When I Am Afraid, I Depend on My Friends* 121
4 *When I Am Afraid, I Remember God's Promises* ... 126
5 *When I Am Afraid, I Worship God* 130

1 & 2 Samuel for Youth

Teaching Youth 135

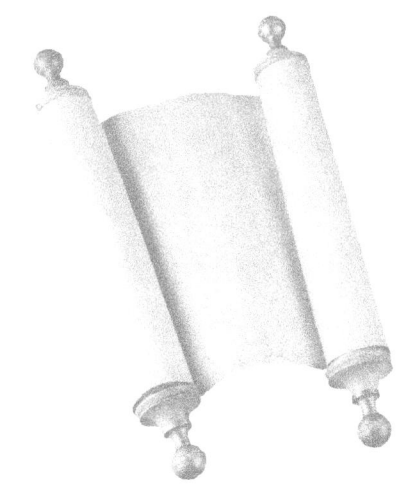

PREFACE

Deep within each of us is a library of stories and songs. Moments of fear, isolation, and darkness drive us to retrieve these literary nuggets from our mind and memory. The emergence of stored prose and poems help move us through tense and troubled times.

As a child, my fear of the dark prompted me to beg my mother for "just one more" bedtime story. She would oblige with a retelling of the brave adventures of Tom Sawyer or Old Yeller or the Hardy Boys. Somewhere between the lines of her neatly packaged narratives, I would fall asleep. The darkness of night surrounded me, but I was safe. Every once in a while, when my wife and children are out of town, I lie alone in my bed—in the dark—and fall asleep with the image of a freshly white-washed fence lingering in my mind's eye.

586 BC was the beginning of a long night of darkness, fear, and isolation for the Israelite people. This approximate date marks the beginning of the Babylonian exile. The city of Jerusalem had fallen to Babylonian warriors. The temple in Jerusalem was destroyed. The sons and daughters of Abraham and Sarah were carried captive to a foreign land. The land promised to Abraham, approached by Moses, possessed by Joshua, ruled by judges, expanded by kings, and loved by all Israel was now miles and memories away. But deep within the memories of the Israelites was a library of stories and songs.

Desolate moments drive us to find peace and hope in the stories and songs that move amid our memories. The books of 1 and 2 Samuel contain a collection of stories (and even a few songs) from Israel's memory that fostered hope for fearful readers. These stories took place in the lives of Samuel, Saul, and David between 1020 and 961 BC. While these narratives certainly have historic significance in the context in which they occurred, their greater significance may be found in the context of when they were recalled, recorded, and retold. In other words, the stories my mother shared with me during the dark nights of my childhood served a purpose beyond their actual historic context and content. They were alive and functioning to bring peace within the contemporary context of a troubled child.

Most scholars believe that the stories in 1 and 2 Samuel were compiled and written during the period of Israel's history leading toward and through the Babylonian exile. More than three centuries after these stories occurred, they were remembered and retold. Why? Why were these stories recalled during the exile? What do these stories say about God and Israel? How did these stories bring peace and hope to the long dark night of Israel's captivity? And is it possible that these stories can bring hope to the tense and tumultuous times of our lives as well?

Sharing these stories and engaging these questions with you is not a task I could accomplish alone. My family—Sonya, Lauryn, Meggie, and Holly—has been supportive and understanding of my self-imposed exile during the completion of this project. The members of my second family—Gerald Carper, Cass DuCharme, Carol Brown, Ruth DuCharme, and Billie Chapman—have been invaluable guides in the respective areas of instrumental music, choral music, educational theory, children's educational resources, and the operation of various office machines. Many others, including the wonderful congregation at Highland Hills Baptist Church in Macon, Georgia, have patiently prayed, encouraged, listened, and dialogued. I am thankful to each of them for being a part of my life story.

Chapter One

GIVING ATTENTION TO TENSION

INTRODUCING THE TENSION

Every great work of art conveys an element of tension. The sculptures of Michelangelo present creatures frozen in motion. The movement is implied but not complete. Muscles are flexed and etched in stone, creating a unique statuesque tension.

In the paintings of Monet, a series of dotted colors collide to present the onlooker with an image of lilies and lakes and meadows. Close inspection, however, reveals a chaos of contrasting shades and colors held in tension by the artist's patterns. The distinct dots of color give the impression of resolution only when viewed from a distance.

This artistic tension is also an integral part of narrative literature. Stories are saturated with romantic, ethical, and spiritual tensions. These tense themes have found themselves embodied in the fictitious lives of Othello and Desdemona, Rhett and Scarlett, Luke Skywalker and Darth Vader.

Michelangelo's *David*
The most famous image in our world of the figure of David is this colossal sculpture by Michelangelo. The contemplative David sees Goliath in the distance and concentrates on the action about to happen. The strain of this event is seen only in the muscles of his neck and his knitted brow. His body is depicted in the relaxed position known as contrapposto that was used in 5th-century Classic Greek sculpture.
Michelangelo (1475–1564). *David*. 1502-04. Marble. 14'1".Museo di Accademia del Disegno, Florence, Italy. (Credit: Planet Art)

Because art imitates life, we easily relate to the tensions contained in sculpture, painting, and story. The tensions expressed in these works of art reflect that which is indigenous to our own human experience. We have come to expect, even demand, this tension in our art. The absence of tension leaves the audience bored and unaffected. Any resolution of the tension renders the art cheap, empty, or at best sentimental. Why? Because the vast majority of the tensions we experience in our lives and in the world are unresolved. Like a classic Monet, they can only be understood from a distance.

Long before Shakespeare, Margaret Mitchell, and George Lucas entertained the patrons of books and box office by exploiting the tragic and comedic tensions of their culture, the writer of 1 and 2 Samuel exposed the existence of these tensions in human life. The prophetic history of Hebrew Scripture does not dreamily begin with "Once upon a time," nor does it sentimentally end with "and they lived happily ever after." First and Second Samuel begin, end, and are filled with the political, theological, relational, and spiritual tensions that saturate and invigorate our existence.

These four "life" tensions (political, theological, relational, and spiritual) will provide our framework for the study of 1 and 2 Samuel. Before addressing the specific tensions, however, there are other general tensions that provide the necessary context and background for our study. These tensions are produced by the history of the text and the characters within the text.

THE TENSION OF HISTORY

When studying the Books of Samuel, we must give attention to the historical settings from which the text arises. Historical tension is generated because two different historical eras must be considered. Readers must keep in mind both the era in which the events of 1 and 2 Samuel occurred and the era in which the events were recorded.

The events of 1 and 2 Samuel occurred from the early part of the eleventh century BC to the middle of the tenth century BC. These selected stories span the era of the judges through the middle of the united monarchy. The period of their historic occurrence, however, may not be the primary key to their intended relevance. A proper understanding of the second historical context is essential to the interpretive avenue we will explore.

The stories in the Books of Samuel were recorded long after they actually took place. Evidence of this later authorship appears throughout the text. First Samuel 25:1 and 28:3 record the death of Samuel, the traditional author of the books. This would prohibit Samuel from having written later narratives from the lives of Saul and David. In 1 Samuel 9:9 and 2 Samuel 13:18, expressions and customs are explained to what is obviously a later generation. Most telling, however, is the repeated use of the phrase "unto this day" (1 Sam 5:5; 6:18; 27:6; 30:25; 2 Sam 4:3; 6:8; 18:18), which implies that the stories were recorded at a much later date than their occurrence.[1] These stories are not excerpts from the daily diaries of their characters. They were not written "as they happened." Rather, the books of 1 and 2 Samuel are part of a larger corpus of material that was compiled no earlier than the period of the Babylonian exile in the sixth century BC.[2]

The Babylonian exile began in 597 BC with the first deportation of Jews to Babylon (see 2 Kgs 24:12-16).[3] The tragic climax of the Babylonian siege occurred in 586 BC with the deportation of more Jews following the destruction of the temple, royal palace, and private homes (see 2 Kgs 25:8-21). This was a devastating time for the children of Israel. After the death of Moses, they had received the land of promise under the leadership of Joshua. For centuries they were governed and protected by God through a series of judges.

In the eleventh century, the children of Israel began to ask for a king. God appointed and Samuel anointed their first king, Saul. He was succeeded by

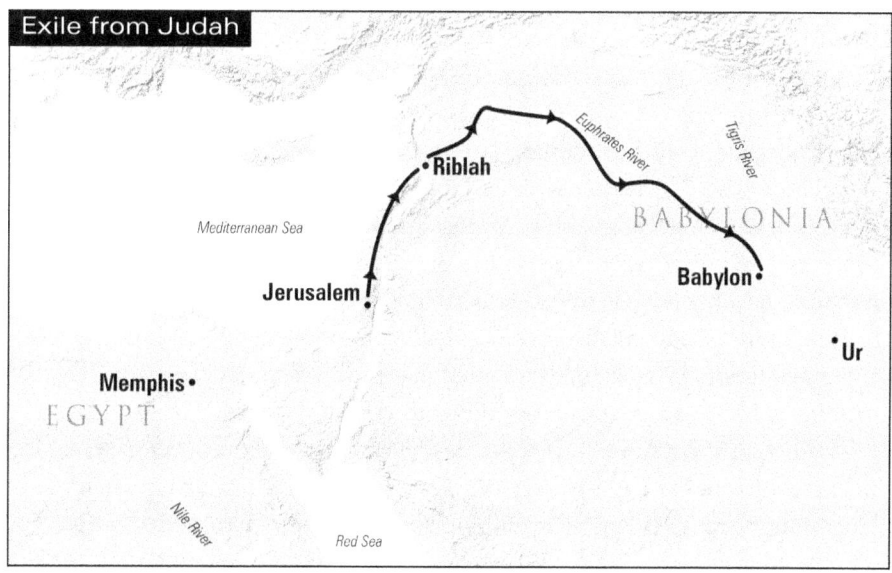

David, who was succeeded by Solomon. After Solomon's death, the kingdom of Israel split. The northern tribes were referred to as Israel and the southern tribes were referred to as Judah. (The city of Jerusalem was a part of the southern kingdom.)

After centuries of divided existence, the northern kingdom was defeated in 722 BC by the Assyrians. The Assyrians did not, however, conquer the southern kingdom. By 597 BC, both the northern kingdom of Israel and the southern kingdom of Judah had fallen to Babylon. A great majority of the Israelites and Judahites were taken into exile.

The Babylonian siege of Jerusalem saw the fall of what had evolved into pillars of Judah's faith: the king, the temple, and the land. The king was defeated, the temple was destroyed, and the land was made relatively desolate. This period of exile lasted until 539 BC, when Cyrus of Persia conquered the Babylonians and began the reintroduction of Jews to their homeland. These years in exile were a time of introspection and self-definition for the children of Israel.

While Jews were separated from their homeland and their temple site, the opportunity arose for the evolution of a new pillar of faith—the word of God.[4] The Hebrew Bible devotes most of its energy to addressing the exilic situation of the Jews. The exile and the "faith questions" it evoked are woven throughout the prophetic and poetic literature of biblical text. From Isaiah to Ezekiel to Lamentations to selected psalms, we hear the questions raised: Is God powerful? Is God faithul? Is there hope? Is there life after exile?[5]

During this period of exile, a collection of books was assembled that retold and retained Israel's history. These books include Deuteronomy, Joshua, Judges, 1 and 2 Samuel, and 1 and 2 Kings. In 1943, Martin Noth proposed that this larger body of material was the compilation of an historian he identified as the Deuteronomist.[6] The Deuteronomist's work helped retain the Hebrew history and culture while the people were enslaved and separated from their homeland. Noth believed these books also presented an interpretation of the exiled Israelites' circumstances. He saw a distinct pattern in the books of God's response to human obedience and disobedience.[7] While subsequent scholars have presented arguments concerning the Deuteronomist's literary parameters and exact dating, it is generally accepted that the audience of this body of material was the exiled Israelites of the sixth century BC.

Simply put, these stories took place in the eleventh and tenth centuries BC but were recorded in the sixth century BC. They occurred during a time when the kingdom of Israel was emerging and growing. They were recorded and read

> **Deuteronomistic History**
>
> Since the publication of Martin Noth's *Überlieferungsgeschichtliche Studien* in 1943, many biblical scholars have adopted his view that Joshua to Kings (with the exception of Ruth) forms a unified literary work. Noth argued that this history was promulgated in the exilic period to explain why the people of God, who had been promised possession of the promised land and a Davidic kingship *forever*, were now deprived of both. In Noth's view, there was a single author of the Deuteronomistic History (DH), whom he called "the Deuteronomist" (Dtr).
>
> This editor is seen more as a compiler than a writer, incorporating earlier traditions—both oral and written—into his work. The Deuteronomist's creativity is seen in his skillful editing of narratives covering Israel's history from the 13th-century BC settlement in Palestine to the destruction of Jerusalem in 587 BC in order to justify his interpretation of the exile.
>
> Noth's concept, though widely adopted, has been challenged on several grounds. For example, Noth argued that the DH had a negative purpose only: to show the history of unfaithfulness that led to the exile of Israel. Subsequent scholars see a more positive purpose. Hans Walter Wolff, for example, sees an implication of hope in the repetition of the word *shub* ("to return" or "to repent"; see Deut 4:25-31; 20:1-10; 1 Sam 7:3; 1 Kgs 8:33, 35, 47, 48; 2 Kgs 17:13; 23:25). As God had restored the ancestors when they "returned" to faithfulness, perhaps God would do the same for the exiles if they did the same. Likewise, Gerhard von Rad found in God's covenant with David (2 Sam 7) and its frequent reiteration in the books of Kings the implication that God would not utterly forsake his people (1 Kgs 8:20, 25; 9:5; 11:5, 13, 32, 36; 15:4; 2 Kgs 2:4; 8:19; 19:34; 20:6).
>
> Noth held that the DH was the work of a single author who publicized his work shortly after 560 BC (the date of the release of King Jehoiachin from the Babylonian prison, which is the last date mentioned in the DH), but before 538 BC (the date of Cyrus' edict ending the exile, an event not mentioned in the DH). Many scholars now argue for at least two editions of the DH, belonging to the preexilic and exilic periods.
>
> For further reading, consult Terence E. Fretheim, *Deuteronomistic History* (Nashville: Abingdon, 1983); Steven L. McKenzie, "Deuteronomistic History," *The Anchor Bible Dictionary*, ed. David Noel Freedman, 6 vols. (New York: Doubleday & Co., 1992; and the discussion of Walter Brueggemann and Hans Walter Wolff in *The Vitality of Old Testament Traditions*, 2d ed. (Atlanta: John Knox, 1982). An English translation of Noth's original work is available as *The Deuteronomistic History*, 2d ed., JSOT Supplement Series No. 15 (Sheffield: Sheffield Academic Press, 1991).

during a time when the kingdom of Israel was exiled and enslaved. Therein lies the tension.

Our challenge is to read these stories through the eyes of the exiled. As David Jobling suggests, these stories are "a national autobiography, developed over a long period of time, out of an acute anxiety about how Israel's present is related to its past."[8] The original readers of these books were not contemporaries of Samuel, Saul, and David who participated in the pageantry of their leadership.

Rather, the implied audience is a population of exiled slaves with only memories of kings and a kingdom to call their own.

It will be tempting to ask, "What did the Israelites think when Samuel anointed the first king?" or "How did the priests feel when Saul broke sacrificial laws?" or "What did David's family think when he committed adultery with Bathsheba?" At every turn, however, we must force the questions to originate from the exiles, not from the characters' contemporaries. The primary question must be, "What did this story mean to an exiled Israelite in Babylon?" It is within that conversation that we will seek to find intent and truth and relevance.

THE TENSION OF CHARACTERS

First and Second Samuel present the reader with three primary characters—Samuel, Saul, and David—whose lives provide the framework for the progress of Israel's story. Each of these characters plays a very distinct role in the story of Israel. Samuel serves as the last judge of Israel and the anointer of kings. Saul serves as the first king and David serves as the first king to garner God's favor.

Though distinct in their roles, the individuals are not examined separately in the text. Their stories overlap within personal relationships and within the text. We cannot conclude the reading of one character's story before the intrusion of the next character. The overlapping narratives result in an inevitable tension.

This literary device is a unique characteristic of the Deuteronomist's structure in the books of Samuel. In the preceding book of Judges, each judge ruled without intrusion from the prior or next judge. The life and performance of each judge was compartmentalized with respect to other judges. In the books that follow Samuel, 1 and 2 Kings, the kings of the divided monarchy reign and rarely influence the kings who precede or succeed them. The tension between characters is uniquely woven into the record and relevance of 1 and 2 Samuel. Some have argued that these overlapping narrative traditions are evidence of multiple sources being "cut and pasted" together into an awkward final form.[9] The sources most commonly identified are pro-monarchial and anti-monarchial traditions.[10] Could it be, however, that this is a purposeful structure intended to produce, or better yet reflect, the reality of tension?

Samuel was a well-respected judge within the theocracy of Israel. No king had ruled over Israel. Rather, based upon the needs of the community and the whim or will of God, judges were called to settle disputes and face enemies. It is during the ministry of Samuel that the people of Israel request—demand—the appointment of a king. Much to Samuel's dismay and surprise, God acquiesces to their demand. While Samuel's life and ministry span chapters 1–18 of 1 Samuel, Saul enters the narrative in chapter 9 and David enters in chapter 16. The last judge and the first kings must coexist in an obvious tension.

Saul serves as the first king of Israel. He is introduced to the reader in 1 Samuel 9 and anointed in 1 Samuel 10. His reign will continue until chapter 31, the last chapter of 1 Samuel. The tensions created by his coexistence with the judge who precedes him and the king that will replace him are obvious. Saul, situated between the greatest of judges and the most beloved of kings, seems destined for failure.

The overlapping character tensions seen in the text are also reflected in the relational lives of these characters. Samuel disapproves of the new monarchy, yet he loves and grieves for Saul. Saul is jealous of David, but David is ironically his source of solace, his greatest warrior, and his son's best friend. Saul seeks to kill David, but David respects Saul in his role as the anointed one of Israel. David flees from Saul on numerous occasions, yet weeps at his death.

One final character who adds to the tension of 1 and 2 Samuel is God. The Deuteronomist seems deliberate in conveying the diminishing role of God throughout the progression of the narrative and individually within the narrative of each primary character. Samuel struggles with the diminishing role of God in Israel's governance as the first king is anointed. Saul experiences the diminishing role of God as the Spirit of God abandons him. During the lengthy narrative scope of the Davidic saga, God is less and less prominent.

Moving further into Deuteronomic literature, the narrative material in 1 and 2 Kings presents God as reactionary. God either rewards or punishes the behavior of kings, but rarely directs the activity of the leaders of the divided monarchy. Prophets like Elijah and Elisha will speak a word for God, but God does not appear to be an integral part of the governance of the people. First and Second Kings moves the history of Israel to the Babylonian exile, where the diminished role of God, God's perceived absence, is most keenly felt.

THE TENSIONS OF LIFE

The aforementioned historic and character tensions will serve as a background for our study of 1 and 2 Samuel. Our primary attention, however, will be given to the political, theological, relational, and spiritual tensions that permeate this portion of Israel's recorded history. Each of these four tensions will be correlated to the life of one of the text's dominant characters. In the stories of Samuel, we will explore political tension. Saul's life will serve as a backdrop for our discussion of theological tension. David will provide an avenue for the discussion of relational tension. And God's role in the text will guide our thoughts concerning spiritual tension.

Samuel — Political Tension

Samuel stood at a unique transitional point in Israel's history. He was the last of the judges and anointed the first of Israel's kings. Samuel served as God's instrument in the movement of Israel from a theocracy to a monarchy—a move of which neither Samuel nor God approved.

The theocratic government that Israel experienced under the leadership of the judges was a purposeful alternative to the oppressive government they had experienced in their past.[11] Embedded in their memories were images of pharaohs, bricks, whips, and forced labor. In this promised land of freedom, they served God and God alone. They paid homage and tithe to God and God alone. Within their covenant relationship with God, they enjoyed the Sabbath cycles of rest, feast days, and an ideal system of economic justice. There was no earthly king or pharaoh to tax or torture or reign as tyrant over them.

According to 1 Samuel 8:10-20, the people settled into their new land and developed a need to be like other nations, to be defended from other nations, and to protect their own economic and political interests.[12] It is Samuel who stands at this political crossroad and personifies the pain of political tension. Samuel has been devoted to the God of Israel, yet he must suffer because God has chosen to endorse the alternative system.

Saul — Theological Tension

If Samuel personifies the pain of political tension, Saul embodies the tragedy of theological tension. Just as Samuel stood at the political crossroads of theocracy and monarchy, Saul stood at the theological intersection of the Mosaic and Davidic covenants.

The Mosaic covenant refers to the relational agreement God made with Israel at Mt. Sinai following their escape from Egypt. In Exodus 19:5, prior to the giving of the commandments and the law, God says, "[I]f you obey my voice . . . you shall be my treasured possession out of all the peoples." This conditional arrangement and the laws that follow provide the paradigm through which God and Israel will experience relationship with one another. It simply guarantees that if Israel is good, Israel will be embraced. If Israel is bad, Israel will be rejected.

At the other extreme is the Davidic covenant. In 2 Samuel 7:8-16, the prophet Nathan conveys to David God's words of promise. Unlike the conditional language of the Mosaic covenant, David and the nation of Israel are assured of God's unconditional love and care. While the Davidic covenant leaves room for punishment, it does not maintain the possibility of rejection. God goes to great extremes to convey the eternal nature of this covenant with statements like "I will make for you a great name . . . I will appoint a place for my people . . . I will establish his (David's son) house . . . and his kingdom . . . forever . . ."

It is the conclusion of these covenant words that demands the greater portion of our attention, however. In vv. 15-16, Nathan shares these words on God's behalf:

> I will not take my steadfast love from him (David's son), as I took it from Saul, whom I put away before you. Your house and your kingdom shall be made sure forever before me; your throne shall be established forever.

This is the deadly and tragic intersection in which Saul stood. Before appointing and anointing the first king, Samuel warned the people in 1 Samuel 12:25, "[I]f you still do wickedly, you shall be swept away, both you and your king." His words were consistent with the Mosaic covenant and they also solidified Saul's pending fate. Saul was chosen by God, just as David would be chosen by God. But Saul did not enjoy the covenant love that would later be bestowed upon David. Saul fatefully stood in the intersection of law and grace.

David — Relational Tension

The first time we laid our literary eyes on Saul, we recognized that his presence filled the room. He was "a handsome young man. There was not a man among the people of Israel more handsome than he; he stood head and shoulders above everyone else" (1 Sam 9:2). When we entered the house of Jesse, however, in 1 Samuel 16, David is nowhere in the room. Jesse has lined up his sons so that the new king of Israel might be chosen, but David is not initially given an audience. After all, he is "the youngest and he is keeping the sheep" (1 Sam 16:11). David is the overlooked child. He is the perpetual underdog. He is the "Cinderella story." Despite David's consistently "weaker" status, he always seems to prevail.

David personifies relational tension. He is the youngest of a series of brothers, each of whom appeared to be more fit for royalty. But David is the one chosen to be king. David is not the offspring of the king, King Saul. Ironically, he is the best friend of the king's son. And David is chosen to be king.

David is a boy who kills a giant. He is a fugitive who is faithful to his pursuant king. He is an adulterer and a murderer who rises through repentance, a foreigner who finds favor with enemies he once slaughtered, and a father who hopes, waits, and weeps for a rebellious child. Throughout the numerous episodes recorded for us from the life of David, we find a man filled with weakness, yet prevailing over the relational tensions of his life.

God — Spiritual Tension

Finally, we will address the arena of spiritual tension in light of the story of God in 1 and 2 Samuel. Of course, God's story begins long before the Deuteronomic Historian puts pen to page. In the days of creation, God is speaking worlds into existence and reaching onto one of those tiny planets to mold humanity from moist soil. In these early days God is busy planting gardens, clothing and marking rebels, sending floods, and dispensing crowds.

God decides to become more personally involved in one family's life and issues a call of promise and friendship to Abram. God perpetuates the promise of home and heritage to subsequent generations. And soon, the family has grown to be a great population of people . . . though an enslaved one.

Again, God is active. He sends a deliverer—fully equipped with rod and frogs and bugs and hail and pestilence and death. God provides clouds, pillars of fire, laws, water, manna, and quail. God provides a land as well as the strength and leadership needed to conquer and maintain it through the ministry of judges.

But one day, the people decide they want a king. God acquiesces, and the more people rely upon the king, the less people seem to rely upon God. God is certainly present with Samuel, Saul, and David. But in the waning words of 2 Samuel, and vividly in the continued writings of the Deuteronomic Historian in Kings, God is increasingly absent. The active God of creation and the exodus has become little more than a supporting character in the drama of Israel.

Theologically, we must affirm the ontological reality of God's presence in the world despite God's absence in the narrative. That is why the final tension is spiritual, not theological. God's absence will be discussed within the context of personal perception, not ontological reality. In other words, the people *felt* that God was absent. The spiritual tension will be more concerned with feeling than logical, systematic thought.

Through the course of this study, it may seem that the political, theological, relational, and spiritual tensions are overstated with respect to their corresponding characters. One might feel that this author has created the concept of each tension and then forced them on their respective texts and characters. While it would be an overgeneralization to affirm that these are the only or even primary intents of the Deuteronomic Historian, it is not irresponsible to allow these themes to permeate our reading of the text.

Remember, we are attempting to read through the eyes of the exiled. The captive children of Israel struggled with political tension—the idea that God had ordained a new system (Babylonian captivity) that was contrary to their prior existence. These same captives struggled with theological tension; they held an inherent belief in their chosenness under Davidic covenant, yet they were experiencing a rejection more consistent with Mosaic covenant. These exiles knew the tension of relationship. They were once again a weakened population of slaves, yet the prophets among them reminded them of their certain deliverance. Even in exile, the Israelites were a spiritual people who experienced spiritual tension; they questioned the presence of God.

When the Deuteronomic Historian presented these stories to the exiled people of God, they no doubt read these stories through the biases of their own tensions. They found their circumstances in the stories. They found themselves in the stories. They found hope in the stories. They found God in the stories. May we unashamedly and perceptively do the same.

PERSONAL PREPARATION

There is no substitute for simply and casually reading the complete text of 1 and 2 Samuel. If you plan to teach, preach, or engage this text in self-study, a familiarity with the whole text will be necessary.

Too often we have allowed others (ministers, teachers, parents, and professors) to select texts from this broad body of literature and dictate our limited contact with its stories and themes. Most people who have been part of a faith community are familiar with a few stories from 1 and 2 Samuel: the call of Samuel, the anger of Saul, David and Goliath, David and Bathsheba, and possibly David and Absalom. The numerous other narrative nuggets that fill these fifty-five chapters are typically ignored.

Attempting to understand these books with such limited contact is like trying to experience tossed salad by only tasting the tomato slices. While the individual stories are rich with meaning, they are only a small part of the message conveyed by the Deuteronomic Historian and received by the exiled Israelite community. A few selected stories alone cannot yield the varied tensions present in the complete text.

If, however, you begin your personal preparation with a casual reading of these two books, you will sense the tension in the narrative that your reading of select texts has likely never revealed. There are few relaxing chapters in 1 and 2 Samuel, perhaps because there are few relaxing moments in exile.

The ultimate goal of this study is to interpret these stories through the eyes and ears of their intended audience—the exiled Israelites. After your casual reading of the complete text, prepare for each individual session by reading the selected focal passage with deliberate imagination. As you read the focal passage, imagine that you are an Israelite slave in Babylon. You are separated from your home, your place of work, and your place of worship. You may imagine that you are a faithful Israelite who has been swept innocently into exile because of the sins of your fellow Israelites. Or you may choose to be an exile who is keenly aware of your own shortcomings. Either will do. This constant imaginative perspective will prevent you from interpreting the text in the era of its occurrence rather than the era of its remembrance, recording, and recitation.

After familiarizing yourself with the breadth of the text and the depth of its audience, you are ready to share the material with your own audience.

PEDAGOGICAL PREPARATION

It is assumed that the reader of this Teaching Guide plans to engage and present the material through the medium of worship or group study. At the end of each chapter, resources are provided to assist in the two different settings.

Guiding the Worshiper

The section titled *Guiding the Worshiper* offers a synopsis of worship theme, a suggested order for worship, theme appropriate musical options, and at least two sermon outlines.

The synopsis of worship theme introduces the intent and focus for the worship service. It reminds the worship leader that "exiled peoples" are the intended audience of these stories. It then assists the worship leader in understanding how the chosen texts for each unit convey a particular message to people who need hope amid their moments of exile.

The suggested orders for worship provide a general structure for the worship experience as well as specific litanies, prayers, hymns, and other elements that may be used in worship. All suggested hymns are selected from the 1991 edition of *The Baptist Hymnal*. Most of the hymns, however, are available in hymnals of other worship traditions.

While these suggested services are more formal or traditional in style, the leader should feel free to shift, eliminate, and add elements to accommodate his or her church's particular worship style. It may be beneficial, however, to use the suggested services even if they differ from your usual format for worship. This could provide an opportunity to accentuate exile. For instance, if your worship style is usually characterized as warm and informal, a more structured service might convey the importance of retaining elements of tradition and culture in the context of foreign exile.

Following the proposed order for worship is a section titled *Musical Options*, which provides a list of appropriate instrumental and choral selections for each worship service. The instrumental music suggestions are organ and piano pieces that compliment the suggested worship theme. They cover a variety of difficulty levels, but again are primarily formal or traditional in style. The choral anthems also follow the suggested theme and vary in their degree of difficulty.

The final portion of *Guiding the Worshiper* contains suggested sermon outlines. At least two sermon outlines are presented for each chapter. One of the suggested outlines is expository in nature. The preacher is encouraged to move through the focal text and allow the elements of that one text to provide the message to the "exiled audience." Expository outlines typically include an introductory remark, an outline of basic points gleaned from the focal text, and a conclusion that reiterates the primary issue addressed in the text and sermon.

There is also a narrative sermon suggestion provided for the worship leader. This outline addresses the focal text in relation to the broader texts addressed in each chapter of the Teaching Guide. This outline is characterized by movements rather than points. Each movement represents a story from the broader texts of 1 and 2 Samuel and is connected to the session theme. These outlines generally include an introductory remark, a brief synopsis of each movement with their intended connection to the theme, and a conclusion that reiterates the primary issue running through the series of movements.

These sermon suggestions are not complete manuscripts, and they contain little, if any, illustrative material. Their purpose is to prompt your thoughts as you prayerfully engage the text in preparation for the preaching ministry.

Guiding the Learner

For those planning to teach the Books of Samuel rather than engage them in the worship setting, each chapter provides a section titled *Guiding the Learner*. This section includes instruction and resources for leading lectures and group discussions of the Bible study materials.

Guiding the Learner is divided into three areas of information and resource: *The Occurrence, The Memory,* and *The Interpretation.* These three sections correspond to identically titled chapter divisions in the Study Guide. This will allow the teacher to use language, material, and organizational terms that are familiar to students who have read the Study Guide.

The section titled *The Occurrence* provides the teacher with information relative to the time in which the events of the focal passage took place. An outline of the focal passage is provided along with other outlines and resource material that the teacher may find helpful in the process of lecturing or leading group discussion.

The Memory addresses the context in which the focal passage was recorded and read. Tensions experienced by Israelites in exile will be related to tensions recorded in the focal passage. An outline of broader texts is typically constructed to show the literary context in which the focal passage is nestled. Suggested activities are provided to help the learner hear these stories from the perspective of the exiled Israelite community.

Finally, *The Interpretation* connects the text to the learner's life circumstances. A series of questions prompts the learner to relate the tensions in the text to similar tensions that are present in their own lives. Some illustrative material is provided to serve as a model for modern relevance.

In addition to the resources found at the end of each chapter, there are also suggested teaching guides for youth and children included as Appendices at the conclusion of this book. Each of these appendices provides a five-session series that can be taught concurrently with the adult material. The sessions do not "build" on one another so the number of sessions can be adjusted to fit your church's class or conference schedule.

Now, let's see if we can "convey the tension" of this introductory material to a contemporary audience.

CONVEYING THE TENSION

Guiding the Worshiper

Synopsis of Worship Theme

Our purpose thus far in the Teaching Guide has been to introduce the Babylonian exile as the context for properly understanding the stories contained in 1 and 2 Samuel. A worship experience based upon this introductory chapter should lead worshipers to recognize and confront moments of exile in their own lives.

In the hour of worship, you may be tempted to reconcile the pain your parishioners experience in their personal exiles. Resist this temptation. It is our tradition, even our mission, in the Christian faith to present listeners with "good news." Personal exiles, however, are rarely reconciled quickly; sometimes they must be endured for a long while. Allow the worship hour to pass and end with no answers provided for the private problems of your congregation. The only hint of reconciliation should be the suggestion of hope. Such is the nature of exile.

Historically, worship elements that question God or raise personal complaints to God have been referred to as laments. Many of the songs and prayers included in the Book of Psalms are laments. They question God about the evil, pain, and suffering that invade the life of the writer or the community of faith. Psalm 137 is a lament psalm that originates in the Babylonian exile.[13] It will serve as an appropriate call to worship in our suggested worship order.

Since we had no focal passage for our introductory discussion of 1 and 2 Samuel, we will use the story of Hannah in 1 Samuel 1 as our primary worship text. This story of a barren woman's lament will provide a personal portrait of an individual's sense of exile.

Suggested Order of Worship

CALLING UPON THE COMMUNITY OF FAITH
Chiming of the Hour
Organ Prelude
Call to Worship   Psalm 137:1-4
Hymn of Gathering   "Come, Ye Disconsolate"   CONSOLATOR
Invocation
Welcome of Worshipers
   Minister: The Lord be with you.
   People: And also with you.
   Minister: Everyone who calls upon the name of the Lord will be saved.
   People: May the Lord hear our cries this day.

(While welcoming worshipers, a brief explanation of the service theme would be appropriate.)

CALLING UPON THE PRESENCE OF CHRIST
New Testament Lesson   John 11:17-35
Hymn of Lament   "Pass Me Not, O Gentle Saviour"   PASS ME NOT
Prayer of Lament
   Minister: O Lord, our world is ravaged by the turmoil of war and hate.
   People: If only You had been here.
   Minister: O Lord, our nation is plagued with poverty, crime, and prejudice.
   People: If only You had been here.
   Minister: O Lord, the Church struggles to maintain unity and mission.
   People: If only You had been here.
   Minister: O Lord, our families and friends have suffered grief, loss, and illness.
   People: If only You had been here.
   Minister: Do you believe that God is present and powerful among us?
   People: We believe. May God's Spirit help our unbelief. Amen.

Adult *Giving Attention to Tension* 23

CALLING UPON THE POWER OF GOD
Hymn of Offering 416   "My Faith Looks Up to Thee   OLIVET
Offertory Prayer
Offertory
Old Testament Lesson   1 Samuel 1:1-17
Choral Anthem
Sermon

CALLING UPON THE REALITY OF HOPE
Hymn of Hope 74   "O God, Our Help in Ages Past"   ST. ANNE
Silent Reflections
Benediction
  Minister: They that wait upon the Lord shall renew their strength.
  People: May we not grow weary. May we not faint.
  All: Amen.
Organ Postlude

Note: If singing the Gloria Patri and/or Doxology is a part of your worship tradition, their absence from the order of worship will help accentuate the sense of exile.

Musical Options

Instrumental Music
  O Man Bewail Thy Grievous Fall, Bach (organ)
  O Lord Be Merciful to Me, Walther (organ)
  Speak to My Heart, Nancy Smith (piano)
  Dear Lord and Father of Mankind, James Pethel (piano)

Anthems
  Go Not Far from Me, O God, Zingarelli, SATB, H.W. Gray Co., C.M.R. 1464
  How Shall I Sing to God, Larson, SATB, Shawnee Press, A 7316
  Psalm 86, Nygard, SATB/Solo, Hinshaw Music, HMC-755

Sermon Outlines

What Pain Produces (An Expository Outline)

There are few pains as severe as the pain of barrenness. Desperately wanting a child and then confronting infertility leads to the private suffering of many couples. The suffering equated with barrenness was even more severe in ancient Hebrew culture. In the minds of many Hebrews, to be barren was to be cursed. This is the pain of Hannah.

I. Pain produces suffering. (vv. 5-7)
II. Pain produces questions. (vv. 8)
III. Pain produces prayerful promises. (vv. 10-11)
IV. Pain produces misunderstanding. (vv. 12-14)
V. Pain produces hope. (vv. 17)

The Israelite, who was struggling to survive and find life in Babylonian exile, felt cursed. What circumstances have driven us to feel cursed, to know pain and to need hope?

Through the Eyes of the Exile (An Expository Outline)

Rose-colored glasses have often served as the avenue for seeing beauty when beauty does not exist. Some experiences are too harsh for rose-colored glasses, however. Such is the nature of exile. When in exile, we see:

I. The Wicked Prosper (vv. 4)
II. Human Pain and Suffering (vv. 5-7)
III. Faith Misunderstood (vv. 9-14)
IV. A Glimmer of Hope (vv. 17)

Did the Israelites encounter in their exile the same issues that were present in Hannah's dilemma? Can we find ourselves in the story as well?

No Immunity (A Narrative Outline)

A popular "reality" television show called *Survivor* rewards its participants with immunity. On each episode, one participant is voted out of the tribe. Another participant, however, has the good fortune of earning immunity. This insures that they do not have to endure the pain of being voted out of the tribe.

In our actual daily living, however, no one is immune to the pains of life. Everyone is either moving toward a crisis or away from a crisis. Everyone is in need of hope.

I. Hannah—A Faithful Wife Is Not Immune to Pain (1 Sam 1–2:11)
II. Eli—A Faithful Priest Is Not Immune to Pain (1 Sam 2:12–4:18)
III. Philistines—Faithless Foreigners Are Not Immune to Pain (1 Sam 5–6)
IV. Israel—An Exiled Nation Is Not Immune to Pain (Relate the context in which Israel read these stories.)
V. Today—We Are Not Immune to Pain (Relate modern examples and our need for hope.)

Guiding the Learner

The Occurrence

The primary purpose of this first chapter is to introduce the reader to the exilic perspective. To understand the interpretive angle of subsequent chapters, readers must be acquainted with two historic contexts: when the event occurred and when the event was recorded.

Learners will benefit from a basic understanding of Israelite history. People often read or hear stories from the Old Testament with little understanding of their sequential place in the biblical narrative. The following outline will help you convey Israel's story in a succinct and manageable manner. Be sure to highlight the fact that the stories of 1 and 2 Samuel occurred during the final days of the judges and the early days of the united monarchy. But these stories were recorded and retold during the Babylonian exile.[14]

A BRIEF HISTORY OF ISRAEL

PERIOD	DATE	RELATED TEXTS	SYNOPSIS
Primeval	c. pre-2000 BC	Gen 1–11	Israel does not exist.
Patriarchal	c. 2000–1700 BC	Gen 12–50	Israel is a family.
The Exodus	1280–1250 BC	Exod–Deut	Israel is a population of freed slaves.

Conquest of Canaan	1250–1200 BC	Josh	Israel enters the land of promise.
The Judges	1200–1020 BC	Judg	Israel is a loose confederacy of tribes united under the leadership of judges to defend against enemies.
United Monarchy	1020–922 BC	1 Sam–1 Kgs 11	Israel is governed by Kings Saul, David, and Solomon.
Divided Monarchy	922–597 BC	1 Kgs 12–2 Kgs	Israel, the northern kingdom, and Judah, the southern kingdom, are independently ruled.
Assyrian Siege	722 BC	2 Kgs 17	Israel falls to Assyria but Judah remains sovereign.
Babylonian Exile	(597) 586–539 BC	2 Kgs 25	Israel and Judah fall to Babylon and are systematically deported into exile.
Persian Liberation	539–333 BC	2 Chr 36:22-23, Ezra, Neh	Cyrus of Persia allows the exiles to return to Jerusalem.

To understand better the tense nature of the Samuel narratives, readers should be acquainted with the overlapping stories of the primary characters. The following survey and outline illustrate the intersection of these prominent characters within the text:

A BRIEF SURVEY OF CHARACTER TEXTS

SAMUEL
1 Samuel 1–25

SAUL
1 Samuel 9–31

DAVID
1 Samuel 16–2 Samuel 24

Samuel and Saul share sixteen chapters.
Samuel and David share nine chapters.
Saul and David share sixteen chapters.
All three share nine chapters.

AN OUTLINE OF 1 & 2 SAMUEL

I. Samuel: The Old Leadership (1 Sam 1–7)
II. Samuel and Saul (1 Sam 8–15)
III. Samuel and David (1 Sam 16)
IV. Saul and David (1 Sam 17–31)
V. David (2 Samuel)

The Memory

In order for learners to read 1 and 2 Samuel from the exilic perspective, they must acquire a sense of the nature of exile. The following activities may help acquaint learners with the possible sights, sounds, and feelings associated with this period of Israel's history.

A Biblical Survey of Exilic Texts
Assign each of these texts to a student in the class. Have them read the texts silently. (If this is a large class or conference, the texts may be assigned to groups.) Instruct the individuals (or groups) to share characteristics of the Babylonian exile evident in each text. Write these characteristics on a posterboard that can be displayed throughout the course of your study.

2 Kings 24:8-16
2 Kings 25:1-12
2 Chronicles 36:15-21
Psalm 137
Daniel 1

Comparing Exilic Experience
In 1971, Corrie Ten Boom published her memories of the Nazi intrusion into Holland and her subsequent imprisonment. In her book *The Hiding Place*, she recalls a truck ride to her first place of confinement. Read the following excerpt and encourage your group to reflect on the questions.

> It was dark night when we were marched at last out of the building. The green bus was gone. Instead we made out the bulk of a large canvas-roofed army truck. Two soldiers had to lift Father over the tailgate. There was no sign of Pickwick. Father, Betsie, and I found places to sit on a narrow bench that ran around the sides.
>
> The truck had no springs and bounced roughly over the bomb-pitted streets of the Hague. I slipped my arm behind Father's back to keep him from striking the edge. Willem, standing near the back, whispered back what he could see of the blacked-out city. We had left the downtown section and seemed to be headed west toward the suburb of Scheveningen. That was our destination then, the federal penitentiary named after this seaside town.
>
> The truck jerked to a halt; we heard the screech of iron. We bumped forward a few feet and stopped again. Behind us massive gates clanged shut.
>
> We climbed down to find ourselves in an enormous courtyard surrounded by a high brick wall. The truck had backed up to a long low building; soldiers prodded us inside. I blinked in the white glare of bright ceiling lights.
>
> *"Nasen gegen Mauer!"*—"Noses to the wall!"
>
> I felt a shove from behind and found myself staring at cracked plaster.[15]

- What sights, sounds, and feelings might the victims of Nazi occupation have shared with the victims of Babylonian exile?
- What specific elements, in the excerpt you just heard, prompted your observations?

The Interpretation
Use the following questions to help your students recognize their own experiences of exile:

- Is there a moment or period in your life that you would consider a time of exile?
- How would you describe your physical, mental, and spiritual state during this time?
- Are there stories or events in your past from which you derive comfort and hope in times of exile?
- What stories or words of encouragement did others share with you?
- Where are you now in this exilic process? Are you over it? Living with it? And how did it change your life?

NOTES

[1] Robert L. Cate, "Samuel, Books of," *Mercer Dictionary of the Bible*, ed. Watson E. Mills et al. (Macon: Mercer University Press, 1990), 792-93.

[2] Ibid., 793.

[3] J. A. Sanders, "Exile," *The Interpreter's Dictionary of the Bible* (Nashville: Abingdon Press, 1962), 186-88.

[4] Gordon McConville, *Old Testament* (Chicago: NTC Publishing Group, 1996), 58.

[5] Bruce C. Birch, Walter Brueggemann, Terrence Fretheim, and David L. Petersen, *A Theological Introduction to the Old Testament* (Nashville: Abingdon Press, 1999), 346.

[6] Tony W. Cartledge, *1 & 2 Samuel*, Smyth and Helwys Bible Commentary (Macon: Smyth and Helwys Publishing, Inc., 2001), 3.

[7] Roy D. Wells Jr., "Deuteronomist," *Mercer Dictionary of the Bible*, 210.

[8] David Jobling, *1 Samuel*, Berit Olam Studies in Hebrew Narrative and Poetry (Collegeville: The Liturgical Press, 1998), 3.

[9] Carol Stuart Grizzard, "First and Second Samuel," *Mercer Commentary on the Bible*, ed. Watson E. Mills et al. (Macon: Mercer University Press, 1990), 269.

[10] Brevard S. Childs, *Introduction to the Old Testament as Scripture* (Philadelphia: Fortress Press, 1979), 277.

[11] Walter Brueggemann, *Theology of the Old Testament* (Minneapolis: Fortress Press, 1997), 600.

[12] Ibid., 601.

[13] Robert C. Dunston, "Exile," *Mercer Dictionary of the Bible*, 276.

[14] Grizzard, 271, 287.

[15] Corrie Ten Boom, *The Hiding Place* (Connecticut: Chosen Books, 1971), 130.

Chapter Two

THE POLITICAL TENSION

SAMUEL: DEVOTED BUT DEVASTATED

Focal Text: 1 Samuel 8:1-22   Broader Text: 1 Samuel 1–15

Several years ago, I was told I needed surgery to repair a hernia. As far as I knew, I had done nothing to cause this hernia. I didn't deserve it. It wasn't my fault. The doctor said there was nothing I could have done to avoid the condition. It just happened. I was an innocent sufferer.

I had never been a patient in a hospital and had certainly never experienced surgery. Upon sharing my planned procedure with our church, I was inundated with stories and testimonies from hernia survivors. They shared with me their memories of preoperative anxieties. They offered stories about stitches and staples and surgical procedures. I was fully informed of postoperative soreness, restrictions, and possible complications. My wife was worried that the graphic nature of these stories were harming me rather than helping me. I, however, found great encouragement in the fact my friends had survived the procedure in spite of the associated pain. If they could get through it, I knew I could.

One of the most remarkable features of the Jewish exilic experience is that it ultimately produced hope and not despair.[1] While our introductory chapter painted a necessary and bleak picture of exile, this portrait of suffering does not eliminate the reality of hope. In fact, the tensions expressed by the Deuteronomic Historian and addressed in the remainder of this book are not presented to accentuate the negative circumstances endured by the Jewish community of faith. Rather, they are presented to remind exiles that God has handled these tensions in the past and God is capable of addressing them again. The stories recorded in 1 and 2 Samuel are often painful, but their purpose is potent. They assure the exile that hope is alive. If Samuel can survive, then so can I.

TENSIONS IN THEOLOGY

Eugene Peterson called it "one of the most change-charged times in Israel's history."[2] The first eight chapters of 1 Samuel are situated between two distinct periods of Israel's history: the period of the judges and the era of the united monarchy. It was a time of transition from the theocratic governance of Israel's past to the monarchial government of Israel's future. For Israel to embrace the monarchy and release the theocracy of their past was more than just a sociopolitical transformation. It was a theological transformation as well.[3]

Theocracy refers to a governmental system in which the leadership is considered divinely inspired. Israel, since their exodus from Egypt and release from the tyrannical rule of a pharaoh, had claimed no king but God. Israel proposed to order its public life under the direct rule of God.[4] The community's words of confession proclaimed God as the sovereign king of all creation and especially Israel. After the people entered the promised land, God chose judges to carry out divine purpose in the life of Israel; they always served at the whim and will of God. These judges no doubt sensed the theocratic nature of their role. This is reflected in Gideon's response to the people when they tried to convince him to "rule over us." Gideon told the people, "the Lord will rule over you" (Judg 8:22-23).

The judges were in no way empowered by the people and in fact were often unappreciated by the populous. There was Gideon, who pared down an army to unbelievable proportions. There was Deborah, a woman. And who could forget Samson—the strong man who inflicted pain on the Philistines and at the same time escalated the Philistine wrath toward the Israelites. The final judges mentioned are Samuel's sons. According to 1 Samuel 8:3, "[they] did not follow in [Samuel's] ways, but turned aside after gain; they took bribes and perverted justice." The judges were not perfect. They quite possibly would not have been rulers of choice among the general population. Yet these were God's chosen instruments, participants in the theocracy and divinely inspired.

Times change, however. The Israelite population increased, diverse cultural groups were incorporated into the society, wealth was accumulated, cities and agricultural centers were established, and all of this led to a need for defense.[5] The loose choosing of judges at the divine initiative of God did not provide the kind of consistency the Israelites felt they needed. And, as previously stated, the upcoming sons of Samuel were not impressive. So the people asked for a king.

The idea of a monarchy was absolutely distasteful to Samuel. It may be that Samuel was familiar with and influenced by the role of kings in ancient Near

Eastern culture. Kings were often viewed as divine figures who functioned mythically to affect the lives of those who dwelt in the kingdom.⁶ This view elevated the human from serving as an inspired instrument of God to sharing authority or at least having influence upon God. This elevated role is evident in the people's request for a king in 1 Samuel 8:19-20. Their request describes the king as one who will govern them, go out before them, and fight their battles. These were the activities of God!

Not only did the proposed monarchy elevate the status of a human being, but it also diminished the status of God. In 1 Samuel 8:7, God tells Samuel that the people have not rejected Samuel, but have in effect rejected God. God interpreted their desire to be loyal to an earthly king as a displacement of their loyalty to their heavenly king.⁷ Their desire to be governed by a human king was a rejection of the alternative covenant community God had established after their exodus from Egypt . . . and their freedom from a pharaoh they had apparently forgotten.

God chose to grant their request. God chose to endorse and even participate in the political system they proposed. Samuel, the devoted judge, stood devastated in this tense intersection between theocracy and monarchy.

TENSIONS IN TEXT

The twenty-two verses of 1 Samuel 8 provide a textual portrait of the political tension that existed in the days preceding the monarchial era of Israel. The first five verses of the text record the people's request for a king, as well as the reasons that precipitated the request. The elders of Israel gather before Samuel and make two observations: he is old, and his sons, who have been appointed to take his place, are not credible.

Some scholars view Samuel's age and his sons' ineptness as merely occasions or excuses for requesting a king.⁸ They propose that the real reasons the

---

Samuel's Sons

Samuel's personal piety is reflected in the names of his sons. Joel means "Yahweh is God," and Abijah means "My father is Yahweh." Samuel's sons are also named in the Levitical genealogy of the Chronicler (1 Chr 6:28). Joel is also listed as the father of Heman the singer, one of those "whom David put in charge of the service of song in the house of the LORD, after the ark came to rest there" (1 Chr 6:31-33). There, Samuel's family is listed as belonging to the clan of Kohathite priests, who had the special responsibility of caring for the ark (see Num 3:29-31; 4:4-15).

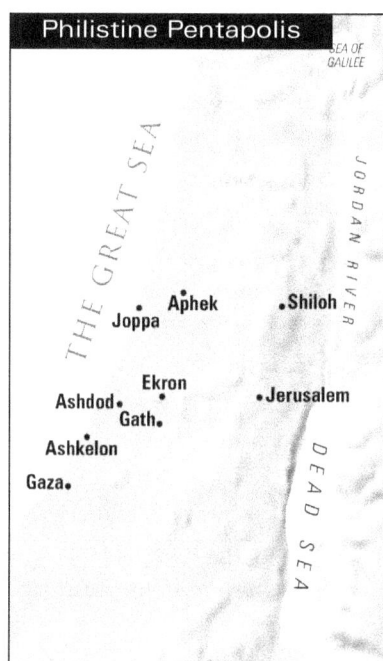

The Philistines

The Philistine population was concentrated around the cities of Ashdod, Gath, Ekron, Ashkelon, and Gaza, though their reach extended much deeper inland. This strong pentapolis of city-states provided security and protection for their inhabitants.

The Sea Peoples brought with them new innovations that provided technological advantages in war. The Bronze Age was drawing to a close, and the Philistines were on the cutting edge of the new Iron Age technology. With their large cities guarding a rather small area, the Philistines were able to muster and train reinforcements for their standing army quickly. Their well-trained army, their superior weaponry, and their reputation as a warrior race made the Philistines a fearsome adversary.

The Philistines were not a long-term power in Canaan, but their influence was so great that the entire area now bears their name. "Palestine" derives from the Latin form of "Philistia" (*Palestina*).

Israelites want a king are expressed by the elders at the end of v. 5 and more fully delineated by the people in v. 20. The elders and people express their desire to "be like other nations" and have a king that will "govern us and go out before us and fight our battles." Recent studies of economic factors during the period of Judges has suggested that the people were beginning to amass wealth and desire more lands for agricultural purposes.[9] A king could provide a centralized government for the tribes, a unified army of defense, and an entity capable of acquiring lands through treaty or military action.

The irony of this request is that it follows on the literary heels of Samuel's successful administration and military victories recorded in 1 Samuel 7, the previous chapter. In chapter 7, Samuel cooperates with God in routing the Philistines (the Deuteronomic Historian's foremost literary nemesis) from the territory of Israel. The victory was so complete that the text records, "the Philistines were subdued and did not enter the territory of Israel; the hand of the LORD was against the Philistines all the days of Samuel" (1 Sam 7:13). Chapter 7 is a clear indication (skillfully placed by the Historian) that God has governed the people, gone before the people, and fought for the people. It would appear that the pre-monarchial institutions were completely adequate and the people's insistence upon change ignores this reality.[10]

With the elimination of each of these excuses, it appears that the only remaining reason for wanting a king is "so that we also may be like other nations." This desire on the part of the Israelites was contrary to their heritage and identity. From this chosen community's inception at Sinai, it has been understood they would not be like other nations.[11] Under the covenant established with Moses, the Israelite people would order their lives according to God's law, live dependent upon God's provision, and trust in God's protection. God is the common denominator in law, provision, and protection. The problem, however, is that God is unseen. God is unpredictable. One must wait for God, trust in God, and threaten enemies with a God that cannot be seen. In fact, the only physical representatives are an aging judge and his less-than-godly sons. As previously stated, their perceived inadequacy provides a comfortable and convenient excuse for requesting a king.

The discussion of Samuel's age and his sons' ineptness, however, may serve as more than a convenient excuse. These verses may indicate that the political tension between theocracy and monarchy were already brewing in the heart of Samuel before it crossed the minds of his contemporaries.

Why were Samuel's sons serving as judges when it is obvious they are not "divinely inspired"? Unlike other judges, we have no narrative of God's call and activity in their life. Instead, v. 1 indicates, "[Samuel] made his sons judges over Israel." The role of Samuel's sons and their flagrant misuse of power appear strangely similar to the narrative concerning Eli's sons in 1 Samuel 2. It appears that two judges, Eli and Samuel, have consecutively extended roles to unqualified children.

Maybe it was Samuel's age, his love for his sons, or perhaps even his personal delight in the wielding of divine power that prompted this nepotistic appointment. Whatever the cause, Samuel, the devoted judge, moved beyond the boundaries of theocracy and apparently followed a practice more monarchial in nature—the paternal passing of power. It is easy to see why the people might feel comfortable asking Samuel about the possibility of monarchy; he and his predecessor had cracked the door.

Regardless of the actual motivation behind the request for a king, God interpreted the Israelites' desire as divine rejection. God assured Samuel in v. 7 that the people had not rejected the role of the judge, but had instead rejected the role of the king as personified in God. God had obviously already been thinking, living, and operating in a monarchial mode. God was Israel's king. They, however, wanted a visible, tangible, manageable king like the other nations. They had rejected God.

God seems to indicate that Israel's request is no real surprise. Israel's rejection of God has been part of a pattern of behavior practiced since the exodus from Egypt.[12] Under Moses' leadership, the people often opted for a king other than God. Whether they were pursued by Egyptians, trapped on the banks of the Red Sea, or existing on the brink of hunger and thirst, they consistently begged Moses to take them back to Egypt. It was hard to trust a God that could not be seen and could not be managed. The unseen God who guided, provided, and protected, was often rejected for a lesser pharaoh. God was not surprised. God was, however, prepared to give them what they wanted.

In v. 9, God instructs Samuel to warn the people to be careful what they pray for. Samuel is to warn the people of the harsh realities of royal power. Walter Brueggemann has called 1 Samuel 8:10-18 "the harshest, most extensive criticism of monarchy in the Old Testament" and "one of the most important pieces in the Old Testament on the abuse of public power."[13] The passage describes in vivid detail the taxation and confiscation that will be a part of this earthly monarchy.

With the business of taxation and confiscation in mind, the primary verb throughout Samuel's speech is "take." It appears in vv. 11, 13, 14, 15, 16, and 17. The king will take your sons for his military and agricultural purposes. The king will take daughters to serve in his presence as cooks and perfumers (a term often used to refer to concubines).[14] The king will confiscate property and a portion of grains and vineyards and orchards and cattle and flocks. The final result of all this "taking" is revealed at the end of v. 17—"and you shall be his slaves."

The Israelites are warned that the monarchy will exist by confiscation and its goal will be personal well-being rather than the welfare of the people. Vineyards are taxed and the proceeds given to the king's courtiers. Grains are taxed and given to the king's officers. Sons and daughters and cattle are taken and put to work in the king's service. Every act of taking benefits the palace and not the people. This practice is in stark contrast to the actions of their rejected God who governed and gave and seemed almost to exist for the sole benefit of the people. The king will place burdens on the people; God lifted burdens. The king will require the people to

> **Palace Provisions**
> According to 1 Kgs 4:22-23, the provisions needed to feed Solomon's court with bread and meat alone for *a single day* amounted to 300 bushels of choice flour, 600 bushels of meal, 10 grain-fed oxen, 20 pasture-fed cattle, and 100 sheep, not to mention unnumbered deer, gazelles, roebucks, and grain-fed fowl. One can only imagine the number of farmhands, butchers, cooks, and attendants required to maintain the flocks and fields and to prepare and serve the meals.

carry him; God carried the people. The people wanted a king to fight for them, but v. 11 reveals that the king will make the people "run before his chariots." God had always fought Israel's battles.

However, Samuel's warning ended not with the descriptive role of the king, but with the changing role of God. His speech ends in v. 18 with the climactic warning, "in that day you will cry out because of your king, whom you have chosen for yourselves; but the LORD will not answer you in that day."

"Crying and answering" had become a recognized form of communication between the human and the divine in the cycle of Israel's faith history. In Exodus 2:23-25, the deliverance of Israel from Egypt is prefaced by the narrator's observation, "their cry for help rose up to God . . . and God took notice of them." In Exodus 14:10, the delivered Israelites find themselves trapped between Pharaoh's army and the Red Sea. Again, they cry out for help and are delivered. The Deuteronomic Historian continues this thematic dialogue as evidenced in Judges 6. When the Midianites prevailed over Israel, the Israelites cried out to God and God delivered them through his servant Gideon. We have even seen the dialogue at work as recently as 1 Samuel 7. In 7:9, in the face of yet another Philistine threat, "Samuel cried out to the LORD for Israel, and the LORD answered him."

Samuel's warning to Israel concludes with the assertion that God will no longer participate in this dialogue of rescue. Israel will cry out, but God will not answer. The people have chosen to substitute human power for the availability of God and they will have to live with the results.[15]

Samuel had done what any good prophet was supposed to do. He had sermonically warned the people of both the physical and spiritual consequences of the present direction of their lives. Israel did what most congregations do; they ignored the words of the prophet. In v. 19 of our focal text, the people reiterate their refusal to give up the idea of monarchy. They rehearse their reasons for wanting a king. They leave Samuel to converse with his God.

After reporting to God his failed attempt to redirect the desires of the people, God instructs Samuel to "set a king over them." One wonders if Samuel was surprised at God's response. Did Samuel's jaw drop, or just his spirits? The judge, who was so resistant, has now been asked by God to be a participant in the political transition. The prophet, who has watched the system of governance he equates with faithfulness fade away, must now help usher in an alternative system he does not trust. Samuel is devoted but devastated.

While our focal text, 1 Samuel 8, is certainly the most vivid example of political tension in the early chapters of the book, it is not the only example. The stories surrounding this politically pivotal moment in Israel's history are vignettes of individuals struggling with their own sense of devotion and devastation. First Samuel 8 is not the only time Samuel suffers as a result of personal devotion. And Samuel is not the only innocent one who suffers. He is not the only child of God who experiences personal exile. Political tension is not something that just exists in the hallways and rotundas of government buildings.

> **Was It Bigamy?**
> Monogamy seems to have predominated in ancient Israel, but the taking of a second wife was acceptable under certain circumstances, such as the first wife's failure to produce children. For example, Abraham took Hagar when Sarah was past child-bearing age (Gen 16:1-6), with unhappy results. Jacob married two women as a result of his uncle Laban's manipulations (Gen 29:15-35), but also had children by his wives' "handmaids" when Rachel and Leah experienced periods of infertility (Gen 30:1-13).

In the broader scope of the Samuel saga, there is a series of stories that reflects this pattern of devotion and devastation. These deep displays of emotional pain are the result of political tensions outside the realm of institutional government. These narratives are testimony to the reality of the politics that exist within the family, the workplace, and even the privacy of our hearts and minds.

First Samuel 1 records Samuel's birth narrative. Samuel's father, Elkanah, had two wives: Peninnah and Hannah. Peninnah had the good fortune of bearing sons and daughters for Samuel. Hannah was barren. Each year the family would make its annual pilgrimage to Shiloh to offer the harvest tithe. A part of this ritual event was the sharing of a family feast (sacrificial meal). It was a joyous occasion for everyone in the family. The father would carve the meat and give portions to his wives and their children. And so, Elkanah carved a piece for Peninnah. And then a piece for each of her sons . . . and a piece for each of her daughters. And then he carved a piece for Hannah. Well, it was a joyous occasion for almost everyone.

According to v. 6, Peninnah "provoke[d] her severly, to irritate her." On the other hand, in v. 8, Elkanah expresses love and concern for her. Neither provocation nor pity could lift the spirits of Hannah. One can only imagine the political tensions at work in this family system.

Hannah's prayers, however, did not go unanswered. Her painful laments to God garnered the attention of a priest named Eli. He mistook her for a drunk and rebuked her. But after being fully informed of her situation, he offered her words of hope.

Hannah had been devoted to her God and devoted to her husband, yet she was barren. In her devastation, however, she was mistaken for a worthless drunk

> **Shiloh**
>
> The ruins of Shiloh are usually associated with the modern village of Khirbet Seilun, a site located in the hill country of Ephraim, 18–20 miles north-northeast of Jerusalem. Although it enjoyed a brief fluorescence as an established cultic center in late pre-monarchic times, archaeological studies suggest that it was not a very important city either before or after that period.
>
> The temple in Shiloh may have been a temporary affair, a sturdy tent surrounded by a courtyard, bearing an altar for sacrifices. The term "house of Yahweh" (*bêt yhwh*, 1:7) could refer either to a tent-shrine or a permanent temple, and 2 Sam 7:6 insists that the ark of God never resided in a permanent structure prior to Solomon's temple (see also Pss 78:60 and 132:7). However, the Shiloh temple is called the "temple of Yahweh" (*hêkal yhwh*) in 1 Sam 1:9 and 3:3. This term is ordinarily used of a permanent sanctuary. If the Shiloh temple was a tent, it may have been similar to these modern Bedouin homes.

and received hope and a blessing. Little did Hannah know that the priest who had given her hope was experiencing an exile all his own.

We met Hophni and Phinehas, the sons of Eli, in Samuel 1:3. They were the priests who presided at the temple in Shiloh where Elkanah and his family worshiped. We meet them again in 1 Samuel 2, where we learn that they are truly two of the most notable miscreants in Scripture.[16] They are described as people who had no regard for the Lord and little regard for the faith practices of the people. While priests were entitled to a portion of each sacrifice, these two men demanded more than the Levitical Code allowed. The Deuteronomic Historian comments in 2:17, "the sin of the young men was very great in the sight of the LORD."

What a disappointment these sons must have been to Eli. As time went on, things only got worse. First Samuel 2:22 states, "[Eli's sons] lay with the women who served at the entrance of the tent of meeting." It is no wonder Eli was present in Shiloh during Elkanah and Hannah's pilgrimage. He may have been attempting to observe and redirect his sons. It is evident in the text that Eli is a man of God; his sons are not. Eli is a devoted priest; his sons are not.

Eli wanted his sons to follow in his footsteps; his sons did not. This devoted priest was no doubt devastated by the outcome of his parenting.

Who could have imagined that Eli would get a second chance? A second chance to raise a child, train up a priest, and see the legacy of his faith continue. The family system to which he had devoted his life had failed. But God provided another young man (through a woman Eli had once mistaken as a worthless drunk) to serve as Israel's next priest and judge and prophet. Hannah brought the son Eli had promised her to serve under Eli in the temple. God's provision had not come through any system the devoted and devastated priest could have imagined. And yet, the young man, Samuel, was Eli's new hope.

1 Samuel 1:10—Hannah's prayer was a bitter but hopeful cry for help.

Julius Schnoor von Carolsfeld. *Hannah's Prayer.* 19th century. Woodcut. *Das Buch der Bucher in Bilden.* (Credit: Dover Pictorial Archive Series)

Chapters 4 and 5 of 1 Samuel provide the reader with a wonderful but messy example of the political tensions that arise from devotion and end in devastation. These two chapters are a part of the sub-source material woven throughout the books of Samuel often referred to as "The Ark Narrative."[17] These stories, which surround the use, loss, and reclamation of the ark of the covenant, seem to have a life and purpose of their own. For our purposes, however, these two chapters seem perfectly placed in their literary context to reinforce the political tension that we have been surveying.

Eli

We know little about Eli's descent or how it is that he came to be priest at Shiloh. The Old Testament does not mention anything about his ancestry other than one reference in 2:27-28, which connects him to the line of Aaron. In competing, though much later, traditions, Josephus assigns Eli to the Aaronide family of Ithamar (*Ant.* 5.11.5), while 2 Esdras puts him in the rival house of Eleazar (1:2-3). Ithamar and Eleazar were two of Aaron's sons (Exod 28:1).

The writers of 1 Samuel are less concerned with Eli's rise than with his fall (along with other Aaronides), and the ultimate ascension of the Zadokite priesthood. Eli's bumbling interaction with Hannah sets the stage for a more extensive description of his incompetence in later chapters.

> **The Ark of Yahweh**
>
> The ark of Yahweh is described in different ways in the various strands of biblical tradition. The elaborate description of the ark in the priestly account of Exod 25:10-22 portrays the ark (*ărôn*) as a rectangular box of acacia wood, about four feet long and just more than two feet square. The removable top of the box (*kappōret*; called the "Mercy Seat," or better, "Place of Atonement") was adorned with two golden cherubim, arranged so that their wings stretched across the top of the ark.
>
> The two tablets containing the Ten Commandments were to be kept in the ark; thus, it was often called the "ark of the testimony" (Exod 25:22) or the "ark of the covenant" (Josh 3:6). These titles focus on the nature of the ark as a receptacle for holy relics.
>
> Other titles emphasize the gilded cover where Yahweh was thought to abide "between the cherubim" (Exod 25:22). Titles that emphasize God's presence include the "ark of Yahweh" and the "ark of Yahweh of hosts, who is enthroned on the cherubim" (1 Sam 4:4).
>
> The ark was thought of as the throne of Yahweh (Jer 3:16-17) or, more likely, as his footstool, the invisible throne being flanked by the two cherubim (1 Chr 28:2; Pss 99:5; 132:7; Lam 2:1). The cherubim were probably winged sphinxes with both human and animal features. In Canaanite iconography, cherubim often flanked the divine throne.
>
> The Israelites believed that God's presence and power hovered above the ark, where Yahweh appeared in a cloud (Lev 16:2) and spoke to Moses (Exod 25:22; Num 7:89). At God's command, they had carried the ark at the head of their procession through the wilderness (Num 10:35-36), across the Jordan (Josh 3–4), and into battle in the promised land (Josh 6–7).
>
> Traditions suggest that the ark rested at various shrines, including Mount Ebal (Josh 8:30-35) and Bethel (Judg 20:26-27), before coming to reside at Shiloh.

In chapter 4, the ark is lost to the Philistines. In v. 18, the priest learns of the loss of the ark, falls over backward, breaks his neck, and dies! It was unbelievable to Eli, and all those who trusted in the power of the ark, that this cultic symbol of their God could be captured. Their system of holy presence and war was devastated. The object of their devotion and the source of their strength was now possessed by the enemy.

It was previously mentioned that this is a "messy" example of political tension. The complexity is due to the fact that the captured ark not only impacted the Israelite system of faith, but it also created tension in the Philistine community. In 1 Samuel 5, the ark is carried by the Philistines to Ashdod, to Gath, and to Ekron. Its seven-month tour to these three locations left fallen idols, hemorrhoids, and death in its wake. In chapter 6, the Philistines return the ark to Israel. The Philistines' faith system, to which they were devoted, has been devastated in the presence of this holy object. It seems no one, not even the foreigners, are exempt from the politics of systemic challenge and change.

Following chapter 8, our focal text, are chapters that overlap the stories of Samuel and Saul. Though the Saul traditions will be discussed more thoroughly in subsequent chapters of this book, we must at least glance at 1 Samuel 15 to see the final moment of political tension in the narratives concerning Samuel.

In chapter 15, God instructs Saul, through Samuel, to destroy the Amalekites as an act of punishment. The slaughter was to be complete. As v. 3 indicates, "do not spare them, but kill both man and woman and child and infant, ox and sheep, camel and donkey." Saul, however, chose to spare Agag, King of the Amalekites, as well as some of the choice oxen and sheep. As a result of Saul's disobedience, God rejected Saul as king over Israel and Samuel refused to accompany Saul further. The chapter ends with a brief but poignant picture of the tension and turmoil within Samuel's heart: "Samuel did not see Saul again until the day of his death, but Samuel grieved over Saul. And the LORD was sorry he had made Saul king over Israel."

It seems that in the end, both Samuel and God had emotionally devoted themselves to a system they originally struggled against, and they found themselves devastated again. Of course, we know there is another king—another system—just over the horizon.

TENSIONS IN LIFE

In the days before the Babylonian exile, the word of the LORD came to the prophet Jeremiah: "I am going to give (Jerusalem) into the hands of the Chaldeans and into the hand of Nebuchadrezzar of Babylon." These words of prophecy are recorded in Jeremiah 32. The fulfillment of this destruction and deportation are recorded in 2 Kings 24–25. The devastation produced by this event became deeply embedded in the conversation, prayers, and thoughts of the captives—particularly those who suffered innocently.

Israel's disobedience and rebellion had led to God's wrath being administered through the hand of Babylon. Not every Israelite taken into captivity could be considered rebellious, however. There were those who could be deemed righteous, yet were swept up in the wrath of God's judgment along with the rest of

> **The Amalekites: A Heritage of Hatred**
>
> Israel had many enemies, but none more despised than the Amalekites, who were purported descendants of Esau through Amalek (Gen 36:12). The Amalekites inhabited the rugged steppes of the Negeb and appear most frequently in the role of an enemy to Israel.
>
> The heritage of hatred went back to the exodus period, when the Israelites were making their way from Egypt to Palestine; they were ambushed by a band of Amalekites who used harassing tactics of cutting off those who were weak and straggling. After a long and bitter battle, Israel prevailed, and Moses declared what he believed to be a word from God: "I will utterly blot out the remembrance of Amalek from under heaven" (Exod 17:14; consult vv. 8-16).
>
> Later, when Moses was giving his farewell speech, he reminded the Israelites never to forget this charge: "Therefore when the LORD your God has given you rest from all your enemies on every hand, in the land that the LORD your God is giving you as an inheritance to possess, you shall blot out the remembrance of Amalek from under heaven; do not forget!" (Deut 25:19).
>
> Amalek's downfall was also predicted by the pagan prophet Balaam, as recorded in Num 24:20. As a perpetual enemy, Amalek was included in several lists of peoples who stood in the way of Israel's possession of the promised land (Num 13:29; 14:25; Judg 3:13; 6:3, 33).
>
> Samuel instructed Saul to exterminate the Amalekites (1 Sam 15:2-9), but he was not successful. Although the text suggests that all were killed save Agag (1 Sam 15:8), the Amalekites appeared again and again. Ironically, it was an Amalekite who mercifully ended Saul's life (according to 2 Sam 1:8-10; but cf. 1 Sam 31:1-6).
>
> David also fought the Amalekites, initiating raids against them, then leading a retaliatory strike after they burned his city and captured his wives (1 Sam 27:8-11; 30:1-20). As David and Solomon consolidated their control over the southern reaches of the kingdom, the Amalekites were forced to pay tribute (2 Sam 8:11-12). By the time of Hezekiah, only a few Amalekites remained, and these supposedly were eradicated by a group of Simeonites (1 Chr 4:42-43).
>
> The Amalekites also figure into the delightful story of Esther, for the hated henchman Haman is described as an Agagite—presumably a descendant of the Amalekite king Agag, spared by Saul but slain by Samuel (1 Sam 15:7-9). Haman is portrayed as one who despised the Jews and wanted to annihilate them all. Haman's heritage helps to explain his enmity for Israel. Nevertheless, Haman failed just as surely as those who came before him (Esth 3–4; 8:2).

their nation. Individuals like Daniel and his three friends—Meshach, Shadrach, and Abednego—come to mind. There were prophets, like Ezekiel and Isaiah, whose words continued to flow during the years of exile. There were children and no doubt others who had remained faithful to their God, and yet found themselves fettered on the road from Jerusalem to Babylon. They had been devoted, but they were now devastated.

The Israelites' devastation may not have been solely a result of their crossing the boundary from Israel to Babylon. More devastating was the reality that God had crossed the boundary. It was clear in the prophetic preaching of Jeremiah and certainly in the minds of the captives—God delivered Israel into the hands of the Babylonians. It appeared that the God of Israel had actually endorsed the rule of the Babylonians. God's choosing of Nebuchadrezzar was as shocking to the Israelites as God's choice of a monarchy had been to Samuel.

The extent of God's relationship with this foreign king must not be understated. A close reading of the first four chapters of the book of Daniel indicates that God was not simply using Nebuchadrezzar as a disposable pawn. Rather, God relates to him in these texts in ways reflective of God's relationship with Israelite kings. God reveals truth to Nebuchadrezzar in dreams, provides interpretation through his prophet (Daniel), rewards the king (Dan 4:2-4), talks to the king (Dan 4:31-32), and punishes the king. There is no doubt that a genuine relationship has been established between the God of Israel and the Babylonian king. God has adopted foreigners as his instruments on earth. And not just for the benefit of Israel, but for the foreigners' own intrinsic value.

Pushing this idea even further into the psyche of the exile is the prophet Isaiah. Chapters 40–55 of the Book of Isaiah are a collection of oracles delivered to the children of Israel while in exile. These prophetic oracles offer hope through the promise of a servant of God who will come and deliver Israel from Babylon. The deliverer is described as "my chosen, in whom my soul delights; I have put my spirit upon him" (Isa 42:1). These words could have well described the deliverers of Israel's past: Moses, Gideon, Deborah, and others who emerged from the community of faith. This deliverer, however, is chosen from outside the Jewish community. Cyrus of Persia is described as the one who "shall carry out all my purpose" (44:29) and "(the) anointed . . . whose right hand I have grasped" (45:1). The exiled Israelites knew the tension of God's endorsement of alternative systems. In fact, the ancient transition from theocracy to monarchy

---

Nebuchadrezzar

Nebuchadrezzar II was king of Babylon from 605 to 562 BC and was the "Napoleon" of his time in that part of the world. He was also famous for his various building projects in Babylon itself and elsewhere (the Hanging Gardens are commonly thought to be one such project). A variant spelling of his name (Nebuchadnezzar) occurs elsewhere (e.g., 27:6-20; 28:11; 29:3). His Akkadian name means, "May Nabu [a Babylonian deity] protect the boundary [or my son]." He gained control of his larger world by defeating Pharaoh Neco of Egypt (and his allies) at Carchemish in 605 BC (referred to in Jer 46:2). Following up that victory, he conquered the Philistine city of Ashkelon in 604 BC (probably referenced in Jer 47:5-7). He first conquered Jerusalem in 597 BC (on March 16 according to the Babylonian Chronicle), removed King Jehoiachin of Judah who had reigned for only three months (see 2 Kgs 24:17), exacted tribute, and placed his brother Zedekiah on the throne. When Zedekiah rebelled, Nebuchadrezzar came against Jerusalem and after a siege of one and one-half years destroyed it in 587 BC (see 39:1-10; 52:4-16).

probably seemed minor in comparison to God's blessing of a foreign system of government.

Our generation is no stranger to the political tensions of life. Our national history is marked with the milestones of transition. We declared our independence from British government. We evolved from a loose confederacy of colonies to a united national entity. We have struggled with the delicate balance between states' rights and national interests. We have chosen to operate within a rubric of opposing but cooperative parties. We are familiar with the tensions of politics.

The political tensions most prevalent in our lives, however, do not occur within the context of government. Our systemic struggles follow the more generalized definition of politics—competition between groups or individuals for power and leadership. These familiar clashes occur within the more familiar arenas of "workplace politics," "family politics," and "church politics," to name a few.

We devote ourselves to a family member, but circumstances or attitudes change. We devote ourselves to an employer or an employee, but transfers, layoffs, personnel policies, or a new employee affects the relationship. We devote ourselves to a doctrine or a diocese or a denomination, but the winds of culture and waves of public opinion (both typically claiming divine inspiration) shift the direction of our beloved families of faith. We are familiar with political tension. We know what it is like to feel exiled. We have been devoted and devastated. But what have we gleaned—what did Israel glean—in the process?

It may be that no one system is intrinsically better than another. Was the theocracy truly more "holy" than the monarchy? After all, there were participants in the theocratic system who fell short of the expected standard. Samson, the sons of Eli, and the sons of Samuel are all evidence of this system's potential for perversion. Instead, the determining factor of systemic acceptability is whether God has supreme access to the system. God appears to be capable of working with just about anyone in just about any situation . . . if allowed.

From this perspective, the pro-monarchial and anti-monarchial materials in the books of Samuel were not recorded in order to force choice. Rather, they have been placed side by side in order to demonstrate that either can be used by God to accomplish divine purpose. While we have primarily engaged the text from Samuel's anti-monarchial point of view (theocracy good, monarchy bad), we would be remiss to forget that both the Davidic kingdom and the Messianic hope and reality emerged from the monarchy. That's not all bad.

So what have we learned in the midst of this political tension?

(1) God cares for those who are devoted to the traditional system of their faith.
(2) God does not abandon those who live within or choose an alternative system of faith expression.
(3) No system of faith perfectly reflects the will of God.
(4) It is not God's weakness but rather God's grace that prompts the divine embrace of our less than perfect systems.

CONVEYING THE TENSION

Guiding the Worshiper

Synopsis of Worship Theme

The books of Samuel are a part of the faith history of God's people. Over the centuries, even millennia, there have been numerous transitions in the method, manner, and place in which this faith and history have been expressed. Prior to the exodus, faith expression in the Old Testament generically revolved around visions, altars, and gifts. Faith expression is more structured after the exodus. The Levitical Codes provided for the celebration of festivals, the offering of sacrifices, and even the construction of symbols and sanctuaries for the practice of such rituals. Later, after the time of David, the cycles of temple building and destruction impacted the modality of faith expression as well.

Christianity has probably provoked the most radical transitions in the worship of the God of Israel. While worship before Jesus Christ focussed on the unseen, mysterious God, worship since Jesus has focussed on God in Christ. Sabbath celebration has given way to Lord's Day celebration. And probably most radical, yet often least noticed, is the transition that occurred in traditional festival celebrations. Pentecost and Passover have undergone a complete metamorphosis.

Passover was originally a celebration of God's deliverance of Israel from the bondage of Egypt. The seder meal, complete with litany and ritual foods, are served and interpreted in light of this pivotal event in Jewish history. At the Last Supper before Jesus' crucifixion, he and his disciples were celebrating the Passover meal. They were sharing the foods and words that had been handed down for centuries. When Jesus blessed the bread, broke it, and gave it to them, nothing seemed strange. But when the words "this is my body" came out of his mouth, everything changed. Traditions were challenged; centuries, even millennia, of devotion were questioned, and a new system of faith expression was ushered into being.

Pentecost, in like manner, had been an annual celebration of the giving of the Law to Moses at Mt. Sinai. The Jewish community was gathered for this celebration in Acts 2. But following the events that occurred that day, just days after Jesus' ascension, Christians transformed the date to become a remembrance of the coming of the Holy Spirit.

Not only has Christianity prompted many changes in the broader history of faith expression, it has also experienced many transitions within its own two thousand-year existence. The Christian faith has grown from a small sect of Judaism to a larger population of European Gentile believers to an institutionalized movement. Within the institution of the church, there arose Western and Eastern traditions. Protestantism emerged from the western Roman Catholic tradition. Within this new freedom of expression, denominations and conventions were birthed. Time has seen each of these Protestant expressions reform and restructure, divide and disseminate. At every turn, for more than two thousand years, there have been political tensions. Systems traded for systems. Devotion challenged, people devastated, faith reinterpreted, and the story goes on.

The following worship experience conveys the political tension of faith history by incorporating several elements from the different eras and families of our faith history. In the "Law" section, a litany from the Passover celebration is included (in English, of course).[18] In the "Prophets" section, the Kyrie is borrowed from the 1961 edition of the *St. Joseph Sunday Missal* of the Roman Catholic Church[19] and the prayer that follows is from *The Book of Common Prayer*.[20] The "Writings" section includes the singing of the Doxology, a congregational response used in many worship traditions. And the "Gospel" section includes the serving of Communion within your church's particular tradition. Alone, each element conveys a particular tension. Placed together, the elements form a beautiful mosaic of the value found in old and new expression.

Of course, feel free to delete, add, and move elements to tailor the service to your congregation's style of worship. Resist the temptation, however, to eliminate all elements that are not within your tradition. You and your congregation will have sadly missed the point—and a wonderful experience.

Suggested Order of Worship

THE LAW
Organ Prelude
Chiming of the Hour
Call to Worship
   Minister: Hear, O Israel: The Lord our God is one God.
   People: We will love the Lord our God with all our heart, and with all our soul, and with all our might.
   Minister: Keep the words that you hear this day in your hearts.
Hymn of Praise 14   "Praise to the Lord, the Almighty"   LOBE DEN HERREN
Litany of Thanks
   Minister: How many are the claims of God upon our thankfulness! Had He taken us out of Egypt, but not executed judgment on them,
   People: That would have been enough.
   Minister: Had He given us their substance, but not torn the sea apart for us,
   People: That would have been enough.
   Minister: Had He torn the sea apart for us, but not brought us through it dry,
   People: That would have been enough.
   Minister: Had He brought us through it dry, but not sunk our oppressors there,
   People: That would have been enough.
   Minister: Had he sunk our oppressors there, but not cared for us in the wilderness,
   People: That would have been enough.
   Minister: Had he cared for us in the wilderness, but not brought us to the Land of Promise,
   People: That would have been enough.
   Minister: Then how much more is the claim of God upon our thankfulness! For He did take us out of Egypt, and execute judgment upon them, and give us their substance, and tear the sea apart for us, and bring us through it dry, and sink our oppressors there, and care for us in the wilderness, and bring us to the Land of Promise.
   People: Bless the Lord, O my soul, and forget not all His benefits.
Invocation

THE PROPHETS
Scripture Lesson   1 Samuel 8:1-22
Prayers of Confession
   Minister: Lord have mercy.
   People: Christ have mercy.
   Minister: Lord have mercy.

All: Most merciful God, we confess that we have sinned against you in thought, word, and deed, by what we have done, and what we have left undone. We have not loved you with our whole heart; we have not loved our neighbors as ourselves. We are truly sorry and we humbly repent. For the sake of your Son Jesus Christ, have mercy on us and forgive us; that we may delight in your will, and walk in your ways, to the glory of your Name. Amen.

Hymn of Assurance 272   "I Lay My Sins on Jesus"   AURELIA

THE GOSPEL
Scripture Lesson   Luke 22:7-20
Celebration of Communion
Choral Anthem
Message
Hymn of Offering 52   "He Leadeth Me! O Blessed Thought"   HE LEADETH ME
Offertory Prayer
Offertory
The Doxology
The Benediction
Organ Postlude

Musical Options

Instrumental Music
   Jesus, the Very Thought of Thee, Colvin (organ)
   May Faith Looks Up to Thee, Mark Jones (organ)
   Take the World, But Give Me Jesus, Rachel Carr (piano)

Anthems
   Devotion, Beck, SATB, Breckenhorst Press, BP1167
   Be Thou My Vision, arr. Parker, SATB, Hinshaw Music, HMC-135
   My Eternal King, Marshall, SATB, Carl Fisher, Inc., CM-6752

Sermon Outlines

Dealing with Disappointment (An Expository Outline)

There are a few "famous quotes" I've heard that make little sense to me. However, one such proverb is "There is no such thing as a problem, only an opportunity in disguise." Another is found in the New Testament book of James: "whenever you face trials of any kind, consider it nothing but joy, because you know that the testing of your faith produces endurance." The implication, however, is that the "end of our rope" is often the beginning of God's new dream. Is it possible this is what the exiled Israelites and today's people of faith need to hear in Samuel's story?

I. Samuel was disappointed in his own limits. (1 Sam 8:1a)
II. Samuel was disappointed in his children. (1 Sam 8:1b-3)
III. Samuel was disappointed in the people. (1 Sam 8:4-20)
IV. Samuel was disappointed in God. (1 Sam 8:21-22)
V. God was ready to do a new thing.

When Faith Crumbles (A Narrative Outline)

At some point in our faith journeys, the spiritual assumptions of our past are challenged. Anchors that have held us fast in days past seem less adequate amid modern storms. Where do we go to regain a sense of perspective and stability when the ideals to which we have been devoted do not appear strong enough to save us from devastation?

When our faith begins to crumble:

I. We go to the house of God (1 Sam 1:1-18). Tell of Hannah's prayers at Shiloh.
II. We go to our friends (1 Sam 5). Tell of the Philistines' moving the ark from town to town.
III. We go to work (1 Sam 7). Tell of Samuel's continued work in light of the information we have concerning his sons in 2:22-25.
IV. We go to God (1 Sam 8). Tell of the people's requesting a king from Samuel.
V. We go on with life. Conclude with Samuel's continued faithfulness to both God and Saul.

God's New Thing (A Narrative Outline)
I. God's "new thing" in monarchy
II. God's "new thing" in exile
III. God's "new thing" in Christ (connect with celebration of communion)

Guiding the Learner

The Occurrence
Since we are dealing with the books of 1 and 2 Samuel with regard to their main characters, it may be helpful for your students to be acquainted with the scope and detail of our first character's life. The Samuel saga stretches across chapters 1 through 28 of 1 Samuel. The first outline provides a thematic structure that highlights the role of Samuel and reflects the primary focus of this chapter—the political tensions between old and new systems. The second outline concentrates on our focal text, 1 Samuel 8.

Thematic Outline
I. Tensions Surrounding Samuel's Birth (1 Sam 1–2:11)
   A. Parental tension (1:1-8)
   B. Priestly tension (1:9-18)
   C. Spiritual tension (1:19–2:11)
II. Tensions Surrounding Samuel's Mentor (1 Sam 2:12–4:22)
   A. Eli's failing sons and Hannah's faithful son (2:12–3:1)
   B. God calling and Eli falling (3:2-21)
   C. Losing the ark; Eli and glory (4:1-22)
III. Tensions Surrounding Samuel's Homeland (1 Sam 5–7)
   A. The Philistines Suffer in the Presence of the Ark (5)
   B. The Philistines Return the Ark (6)
   C. The Philistines Suffer under the Prayers of Samuel (7)
IV. Tensions Surrounding Samuel's Role (1 Sam 8–12)
   A. The people demand a king (8)
   B. Samuel finds the king (9)
   C. Samuel anoints a king (10)
   D. The people confirm the king (11)
   E. Samuel preaches to people and king (12)
V. Tensions Surrounding Samuel and Saul (1 Sam 13–28)
   A. Samuel predicts the fall of Saul (13)
   B. Samuel regrets the rule of Saul (15)

C. Samuel anoints the successor of Saul (16)
   D. Samuel dies in the shadow of Saul and David (25)
   E. Samuel's ghost predicts the death of Saul (28)

Focal Outline: 1 Samuel 8
I. The Limits of an Old System (vv. 1-3)
   A. Age (v. 1)
   B. Human injustice (vv. 2-3)
II. The Demand for a New System (vv. 4-5)
III. The Prayer of an Old Prophet (vv. 6-9)
   A. Samuel's pain (v. 6)
   B. God's pain (vv. 7-9)
IV. The Preaching of an Old Prophet (vv. 10-18)
   A. Practical warning (vv. 10-17)
   B. Spiritual warning (v. 18)
V. The Embrace of a New System (vv. 19-22)
   A. The word of the people (vv. 19-21)
   B. The word of the Lord (v. 22)

The Memory
The following activities are designed to help learners experience the stories of Samuel from the perspective of the Israelite exile. "Experiencing the Broader Text" asks learners to relate the political tensions of Israel's exile to the political tensions in Samuel's life. "Experiencing a Related Text" asks learners to imagine Israel's political tensions in light of Babylon's (an alternative governmental system) relationship to God.

Experiencing the Broader Text
As the captive Jews struggled with their past devotion and present devastation, these stories became their sources of hope. Depending on the size of your class, assign the following stories to individuals or small groups. (If you are lecturing to a large audience, you may wish to tell each story briefly or assign texts to sections of the congregation.) After reading the brief vignettes, have them share their responses to the questions that follow.

1 Samuel 1:1-20
1 Samuel 2:22–3:1
1 Samuel 4
1 Samuel 8

- How do you think the main character of each story feels about God?
- How might the children of Israel have seen themselves in this story?
- What feelings and frustrations were similar?
- In what ways would this story define or provoke tension in the exile's life?
- How would this story be a source of hope for the exile?

Experiencing a Related Text

The Book of Daniel conveys stories that occurred during the Babylonian exile. Chapters 1–4 of Daniel contain stories specific to the relationship of King Nebuchadnezzar with Daniel and Daniel's God. It is evident from the text that God has chosen to engage in a relationship with Nebuchadnezzar. Have individuals or groups review the texts listed below and answer the questions that follow:

Daniel 2:46-49
Daniel 3:28–4:3
Daniel 4:29-37

- What confessions did Nebuchadnezzar make concerning the God of Israel?
- What events precipitated these confessions?
- How do we know God is interested in the life of Nebuchadnezzar?
- Is Nebuchadnezzar truly interested in the God of Israel?
- What would an exiled Israelite infer from the apparent relationship between God and Nebuchadnezzar? How might they feel?
- How might an Israelite assimilate those inferences into their belief system?

The Interpretation

Having surveyed vignettes from 1 Samuel that illustrate the political tensions produced by shifts in faith and governmental systems, learners are now ready to review areas where these tensions exist in their own lives and histories. Read the following sketches and lead the group in answering the questions that follow.

Our National History
State Representatives arrived in Philadelphia on May 25, 1787, to convene the Constitutional Convention. These representatives from most of the thirteen original states met to revise the Articles of Confederation. Primarily successful farmers and businessmen, they felt that commerce and culture would thrive under a more centralized government, in comparison to their present loose confederation of states. The Constitution of the United States of America was birthed at this gathering.

Our Faith History
On October 31, 1517, Martin Luther nailed to the door of the Castle Church in Wittenberg his 95 Theses against the sale of indulgences. This date marks the traditional beginning of the Protestant Reformation.

- How would you describe people's devotion to the "old" systems in each of the above sketches?
- What difficulties or tensions were involved in embracing "new" systems?
- Where do the participants see God in each of these transitions?
- Where do you see God in each of these transitions?
- What moments in your life or in the life of your church would be reflective of such transition and tension?
- Is it possible that God can be active in old and new systems? How?

NOTES

[1] Bruce C. Birch, Walter Brueggemann, Terrence E. Fretheim, and David L. Petersen, *A Theological Introduction to the Old Testament* (Nashville: Abingdon Press, 1999), 350.

[2] Eugene H. Peterson, *First and Second Samuel* (Louisville: Westminster John Knox Press, 1999), 31-32.

[3] Birch et al., 219.

[4] Walter Brueggemann, *Theology of the Old Testament* (Minneapolis: Fortress Press, 1997), 600.

[5] Birch et al., 216.

[6] Brevard S. Childs, *Biblical Theology of the Old and New Testaments, Theological Reflection on the Christian Bible* (Minneapolis: Fortress Press, 1992), 152.

[7] Birch et al., 229.

[8] P. Kyle McCarter Jr., *I Samuel*, The Anchor Bible (New York: Doubleday, 1980), 160.

[9] Birch et al., 216.

[10] McCarter, 160.

[11] Walter Brueggemann, *First and Second Samuel*, Interpretation, A Bible Commentary for Teaching and Preaching (Louisville: John Knox Press, 1990), 62.

[12] Ralph W. Klein, *I Samuel*, Word Biblical Commentary (Waco: Word, Incorporated, 1903), 75.

[13] Brueggemann, *Samuel*, 63.

[14] Klein, 77.

[15] Brueggemann, *Samuel*, 65.

[16] Tony W. Cartledge, *1 & 2 Samuel*, Smyth and Helwys Bible Commentary (Macon: Smyth and Helwys Publishing, Inc., 2001), 51.

[17] Ibid., 69.

[18] Nahum N. Glatzer, ed., *The Passover Haggadah* (New York: Schocken Books, 1981), 53-55.

[19] Hugo Hoever, *Saint Joseph Continuous Sunday Missal* (New York: Catholic Book Publishing Co., 1961), 734.

[20] *The Book of Common Prayer* (New York: Oxford University Press, 1979), 127.

Chapter Three

THE THEOLOGICAL TENSION

SAUL: CHOSEN BUT CHASTISED

Focal Text: 1 Samuel 13:1-14   Broader Text: 1 Samuel 9–15

My grandmother was fond of advising her grandchildren on how to survive in the real world. A woman with little formal education, she transmitted truth to us through proverbial phrases. They are no doubt the same proverbial phrases everyone's grandparents passed along. I don't have to quote them for you. You already know about "birds of a feather," "old dogs" and "he who hesitates."

When my grandmother learned that I felt called to ministry, a new piece of proverbial advice made its way into her repertoire. Concerned for my future well-being, she would shake her head and warn me, "There are two things you should never talk about in public: politics and religion. Son, you're going to have a tough life."

My grandmother knew that the tensions of politics and faith cut deep into the psyche of most people. The Deuteronomic Historian probably knew it as well. But rather than avoid the issues, the Historian allows these realms of tension to take center stage in the early pages of 1 and 2 Samuel. In the narratives surrounding the life of Samuel, we saw the tensions of politics. In the stories that convey the actions of Saul, the first king of Israel, we will see the tension of theology. Thus, in two chapters, we will have surveyed and discussed the "two taboos." I'm not sure my grandmother would be pleased.

For the exiled Israelites, however, the conversations were necessary. The shift in governmental power had certainly raised questions about God's rule in the world. The fact they were exiled and suffering raised further questions about God's role in their lives.

TENSIONS IN THEOLOGY

Theocracy and monarchy served as the stereotypical extremes of the political tension found in Samuel's story. These two governmental concepts could not be easily separated or sanctified, however. We found that each were valuable to the purposes of God. Neither was complete without some hint of the other. Theocracy hailed the God of Israel as its monarch and monarchy allowed the theocratic rule of God to choose its king. Samuel simply stood in the tension produced by these coexisting systems. He stood in the transitional moment between shifts in the "dominance" of a particular system—prior to Samuel, theocracy was dominant and after Samuel, monarchy was dominant. But neither system existed without an intrinsic hint of the other.

This is also true of the concepts of law and grace. These two theological concepts are not easily separated or sanctified. Neither is complete without some intrinsic hint of the other. Both are valuable to the purposes of God and coexist within the nature of God. These are the stereotypical extremes that produce theological tension in the Saul narratives.

While Samuel stood at the intersection of two political systems vying for dominance, Saul stands between two theological covenants that competitively coexist. The covenant within which Saul experienced and expressed faith was the Mosaic covenant. The primary clause of this covenant is recorded in Exodus 19:5. God communicates with Israel through words Moses speaks: "if you obey my voice and keep my covenant, you shall be my treasured possession out of all the peoples."

The Mosaic covenant was primarily legal in nature. Although this conditional statement certainly carried elements of relationship within its linguistic structure, it was primarily defined by law. The chapters that follow Exodus 19, in Exodus and Leviticus, spell out what it means to "obey [God's] voice." To be God's treasured possession involved the embrace and practice of certain moral, ethical, and ecclesiastical obligations.

In comparison, the Davidic covenant was primarily "relational" in nature. The words of this covenant are recorded in 2 Samuel 7:12-16. In this text, God promises David, through the prophet Nathan, "I will raise up your offspring after you . . . . I will establish the throne of his kingdom forever. . . . When he commits iniquity, I will punish him . . . . But I will not take my steadfast love from him, as I took it from Saul." While the legal aspect of a conditional covenant is mentioned, it does not take precedent over the relational aspect of the covenant. Saul's experience was just the opposite. In fact, God acknowledges there is a difference in the covenantal relationship experienced by Saul and the convenantal relationship of those who will rule after him. Saul lived under a covenant in which God's love was "more conditional" than the covenant experienced by David and his offspring.

Some scholars have cautioned against pushing the distinction of conditionality too far. They consider it misleading to suggest that the conditional and unconditional aspects of God's covenants with Israel can be separately analyzed.[1] This caution is well-founded. As already stated, both covenants carry elements of law and grace. The Mosaic covenant is given to a people that are "chosen" and continue to be cared for even when they disregard the law. The Davidic covenant is quick to assert that iniquities will not be overlooked; punishment will be dispensed. Neither of these covenants can be rendered completely conditional or unconditional.

However, it is obvious, perhaps painfully obvious to Saul, that God's covenant relationships are "weighted" toward either law or grace. We can see this bias as we compare events in the lives of Saul and David. We can see this bias in the wording of the covenants. Even God admits the bias when it is stated: "I will not take my steadfast love from him, *as I took it from Saul.*" Therein lies the tension. Those who serve under the Davidic covenant will enjoy a certainty of relationship that Saul did not enjoy.

Saul sits on the fateful bridge that moves Israel from a covenant relationship dominated by justice to a covenant relationship dominated by grace. On the one hand, Saul, like David who will follow him, enjoys the privilege of being chosen. On the other hand, Saul must reign under the justice of the Mosaic covenant—a fate David will, to a great degree, be spared.

Saul was chosen but chastised. He was anointed king, but never really had a chance to succeed. Old Testament scholar Brevard Childs wrote, "Saul's kingship was a false start from the beginning . . . and therefore could not endure."[2] Pastor and professor Eugene Peterson compares Saul to Judas.[3] Both men were chosen, yet both seemed to operate within a theological system that made their dooms inevitable. Strangely enough, both lives ended in suicide.

TENSIONS IN TEXT

First Samuel 13:1-14 is certainly not the most tragic of Saul's blunders. Nor is it a climactic blunder in the scope of his story. Chapter 13 serves as our focal text because it is the beginning of his blunders. The short path of success Saul has been walking leads to a dead end and a steep cliff. Chapter 13 is the fateful bend in the road.

The text begins with the Deuteronomic Historian's formulaic reference to chronology. This pattern of speech will be seen with regard to subsequent kings and their terms of office, particularly throughout the books of 1 and 2 Kings. This first use of the royal formula is a bit unique, however. The actual age of Saul is not mentioned in the Hebrew text and there is some question concerning the accuracy of the length of Saul's reign.[4]

> **Geba, Gibeah, and Gibeon**
> There seems to be some confusion in the text regarding these place names, and no real scholarly consensus for solving it. The problem stems from the fact that all of the names derive from the Hebrew appellative meaning "hill." There are many notable hills in Palestine, and there were certainly several towns or villages named after their physical surroundings.
>
> First Sam 13 refers to a place called Geba, which was apparently located about eight miles north-northeast of Jerusalem, near the edge of the deep and rugged Wadi Sunweinit, across from Michmash. This seems to have been the site of a Philistine outpost that was conquered by Jonathan and later used as an Israelite base of operations (1 Sam 13:3, 16).
>
> The most prominent Gibeah was located about six miles north-northwest of Jerusalem, in the heart of the tribal territory assigned to Benjamin (modern-day Jeba). This Gibeah was named in the tribal allotment lists (Josh 18:28) and was the site of the infamous rape of the Levite's concubine that led to intertribal warfare (Judg 19–21).
>
> Gibeah was King Saul's home town (1 Sam 11:4) and eventually became his capital (1 Sam 22:6; 23:19). In 1 Sam 13–14, Gibeah (along with Geba) figured into Saul's initial conflict with the Philistines. Some scholars regard Gibeah and Geba as identical towns with different spellings preserved by variant traditions underlying the final history. Others prefer to think of two places near each other, while others confess the inability to tell when the text means "Gibeah" and when it means "the hill."
>
> Another Gibeah, located west of Jerusalem near Kiriath-jearim, hosted the ark for a period of time (1 Sam 7:1-3; 2 Sam 6:1-3). The city of Gibeon lay northwest of Jerusalem. It also figured prominently in the stories of the Israel's early monarchical years (2 Sam 2:12-19; 22:1-2; 1 Kgs 3:8-15).

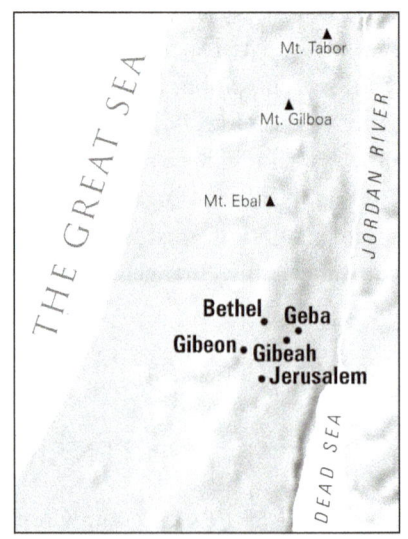

Details within the text get more confusing in vv. 2-3, with the mention of Jonathan's presence at Gebeah and Geba. The Hebrew root of this particular place name means "hill." Since there are many notable hills in the region of Palestine and since many cities were named for the physical nature of their surroundings, scholars have found it difficult to reach a consensus on exactly which towns are referenced and where they were located. At least three different locations within a few miles of Jerusalem could be the site to which the narrator refers.[5]

The narrator's mention of chronological and geographical references may have little to do with precise detail and much more to do with staging. Saul began his reign in the context of war. This is conveyed to the reader through a record of troop movements and battle locations. In chapter 11, Saul's public coronation was precipitated by a military victory over the Ammonites. In v. 3 of our text, Jonathan defeated a garrison of the Philistine army at Geba. In v. 4, war was declared against the Philistines; Israel gathered its troops at Gilgal and the Philistine troops were gathered at Michmash. The stage is set for Saul to do what Saul does best; he is a warrior.

The stage is also set, however, for the testing of Saul's faith. The narrator is hardly interested in the details of military maneuvers or the terrain over which they traversed. Rather, the writer is assuring the readers that faith is lived or lost in the real world—a world that can be described in terms of place and movement and statistics.[6]

In vv. 6-7, we find the Israelites fearful but faithful. Realizing they are far outnumbered, they hide under the leadership of Saul. After all, this is God's chosen king. The enemies are the same Philistines Samuel had handily subdued in chapter 7. And speaking of Samuel, he is expected to arrive any minute and offer sacrifices to insure a successful military venture. At the end of v. 7, the people are trembling, but they are trusting.

Philistine Chariot
(Illustration Credit: Barclay Burns)

After seven days of enemy avoidance, the internal tide of morale began to turn. According to v. 8, a prior arrangement had been made for Samuel to arrive within a seven-day window. At the end of seven days, when Samuel had not shown, the brave soldiers began to "slip away from Saul."

In an effort to maintain troop loyalty and appease the ritual demands of God, Saul performed the priestly task of presenting the burnt offering and peace offering to God. According to Levitical law, the burnt offering served as a medium for petition and purification, while the peace offering promoted a sense of unity between God and those making the sacrifice.[7] Each of these faith elements—petition, purification, and unity—were essential in Israel's ritual preparation for war.

Verse 10 indicates that "As soon as [Saul] had finished offering the burnt offering, Samuel arrived." Whatever confrontation Saul had expected with the Philistines, it probably paled in comparison to the reception he received from Samuel. Saul moves toward Samuel intending to bless (salute) him; Samuel intends to bless Saul out! Samuel raises a harsh and accusatory question concerning Saul's offer of the sacrifice. Saul responds, however, with a reasonable explanation. In vv. 11-12, he explains the scattering of the troops, the need for proper religious ritual, and the tardiness of Samuel's appearance. Saul's reasons were pragmatic, religious, and valid.[8]

Some commentators have been quick to accuse Saul of disobedience to God and disregard for sacred ritual. They have argued that only a priest was allowed to offer these sacrifices to God. They contend Saul overstepped the boundaries of Mosaic Law and rightfully incurred the wrath of Samuel and God. They describe Saul's offering of the sacrifice as an act of disobedience disguised as an act of worship—an act that demonstrated in the minds of some that Saul had forgotten God.[9] But is this consistent with the text? Is this consistent with Saul's stated motivation and subsequent explanation to Samuel? Did Saul act out of disregard for God or out of great regard for God? Was Samuel angry because Saul had disrespected God, or was Samuel angry that Saul had disrespected Samuel?

Other scholars have noted that, in light of the situation, it appears Saul made a sound decision.[10] Saul had not offered the sacrifices hastily. His patience and respect for the priestly ritual is well documented in the text. He simply refused to lose more of his troops and he refused to enter battle unconsecrated. When Samuel's promised moment of appearance came and went, Saul exercised his "God-chosen" role as leader of Israel and sacrificed to God. These hardly sound like the actions of a man who has forgotten God or lost all regard for God. Just the opposite! Saul is acting out of a deep regard for the necessary presence of God.

Was Saul's offering of the sacrifice an inappropriate intrusion into the sacred realm? This notion of cultic infringement by a king has very little substance when compared to God's acceptance of the sacrificial participation of later kings. Both David and Solomon offered acceptable sacrifices to God outside the purview of Israel's priests. (2 Sam 6:17f; 24:25; 1 Kgs 3:3f).[11]

Again, is the real issue Saul's disobedience and disrespect for God or his perceived disobedience and disrespect for Samuel? From Samuel's perspective, it would appear that Saul decided he could function without Samuel. Up until now, Samuel had been active in searching for, anointing, and blessing Saul. Arriving late, however, Samuel is confronted with the reality that Saul (and life) has gone on without him. For a man who has already struggled through the tensions produced during political transition, this was the last straw.

In v. 13, Samuel ignores Saul's explanation for proceeding with the sacrifice and quickly levies accusations and judgments against Saul. Samuel accuses, "you have done foolishly" and "you have not kept the commandment of the LORD." Neither of these charges seems legitimate, however. Saul's actions were hardly foolish. Samuel apparently did not choose to hear the realistic and reverent reasons offered for the apparent offense. As to the unkept commandment of the Lord, Samuel cites no commandment that has been broken. It is impossible for us legitimately to construe such a commandment. In the words of Walter Bruggemann, "The commandment that seems to be broken is—Thou shalt not violate Samuel's authority."[12]

Following the accusations, Samuel pronounces the verdict. Saul's kingdom (which would have been established forever) will not continue and God is seeking a "player to be named later" to take Saul's place.[13] This up and coming king will be a "man after [God's] own heart" and has already been appointed. Again, Samuel's words lack a logical sense of legitimacy. Until this point, Saul has not been informed that his kingdom may have continued forever, nor was he informed that the offering of particular sacrifices were conditions of this kingdom legacy.[14] And at what point had God appointed this new ruler over Israel? Samuel is clear that the new appointment is a divine reaction to Saul's offering of the ritual sacrifices. Yet he also implies this appointment is a completed deal.

If the appointment was made before Saul's infraction, as Samuel seems to suggest, then the continuance of Saul's kingdom was never a real possibility. If the continuance of the kingdom was a real possibility, but was based upon Saul's absolute adherence to all Mosaic Law, then it was not remotely probable. The deck is stacked against Saul, Samuel is dealing, and the next king is sure to get the better hand.

Perhaps the most illogical facet of Samuel's speech is not contained in its words, but rather its timing. Lest we forget, it was Samuel who was late for the

Saul's Activities

In considering the length of Saul's reign, it is helpful to review the major events of his life, as recorded in 1 Samuel:

1. Saul seeks lost donkeys and finds a kingdom (9:1–10:16).
2. Saul is chosen by lottery at Mizpah (10:17-27).
3. Saul rouses Israel, defeats the Ammonites, and is confirmed as king (11:1-15).
4. Saul and Jonathan lead Israel against the Philistines (13:1–14:52).
5. Saul defeats the Amalekites, but angers Samuel (15:1-35).
6. Saul suffers from an evil spirit and is comforted by David's music (16:14-23).
7. Saul faces the Philistines, but David fights Goliath (17:1-58).
8. Saul grows jealous of David and tries to kill him (18–20).
9. Saul hunts David: several encounters (21–26).
10. Saul seeks advice from Samuel's ghost before battling the Philistines (28).
11. Saul and three of his sons die in battle with the Philistines (31).

ritual sacrifice. It was Samuel who did not meet the deadline for preparing God's army for war. It was Samuel who scurried in at the last minute and expected to be forgiven for his disregard and disobedience. Yes, disobedience. If Saul was disobedient for sacrificing after the deadline, surely Samuel was disobedient for missing the deadline! The priest wishes to live according to grace while he expects the king to live according to law.

The fact is, Samuel was never supportive of Saul. In these early chapters of Saul's reign, Samuel's allegiance is half-hearted and his assistance is absent. Samuel was the closest thing to an expert in governmental administration that existed in Israel. But Samuel backed away from Saul and insured his failure. Rather than struggle with Saul, Samuel let him struggle alone. Finally, Saul makes a decision that Samuel is able to interpret as inadequate and Samuel uses the occasion to pronounce judgment on Saul. Given Saul's gracious greeting of Samuel on this particular day, one can only imagine how betrayed and undermined Saul felt when the day ended.

As earlier stated, 1 Samuel 13 is not a record of the worst of Saul's blunders nor the climax of Saul's blunders. Within the literary structure of the Saul narratives, it serves as the beginning of Saul's demise. It is the first of three narratives, recorded in chapters 13–15, that chronicle the downward spiral of Saul's favor. These stories are structurally reflective of three prior stories recorded in chapters 9–11 that chronicle Saul's ascent to the throne.

In 1 Samuel 9, the prophet Samuel is given instructions concerning the location of the one who "will save my people from the Philistines; for I have seen the suffering of my people, because their outcry has come to me." These words of God to Samuel are reminiscent of those spoken during the call of Moses in Exodus 3. There is no doubt that God is taking the appointment of the king

1 Samuel 9:26-27—Samuel anoints Saul as king. Samuel first anointed Saul in a private ceremony outside an unnamed city in the "land of Zuph."

Julius Schnoor von Carolsfeld. *Samuel Anoints Saul as King*. 19th century. Woodcut. *Das Buch der Bucher in Bilden*. (Credit: Dover Pictorial Archive Series)

seriously. Despite God's earlier reservations when Israel demanded a king, the role given to Saul is obviously a positive one.[15]

First Samuel 10 relates the second story of Saul's confirmation. The chapter begins with the anointing of Saul by Samuel. While this act was a symbolic expression of the conveyance of God's blessing on Saul, later verses in the chapter record a more literal conveyance of God's power and presence. As Samuel had accurately prophesied, Saul met a band of prophets from Gibeah (10:10). During this encounter, "the spirit of God possessed (Saul), and he fell into a prophetic frenzy." God had not only called Saul as king, but had now filled him with prophetic spirit.

Finally, in 1 Samuel 11, Saul hears that the people of Jabesh-Gilead are being attacked by the Ammonites. In v. 6, Saul is empowered by God's spirit, his anger is kindled, and he achieves a great military victory. At the conclusion of the battle, Saul gives God the glory for the deliverance and the people affirm

Saul for a job well done. Ironically, it is Samuel who suggests a celebration and reaffirmation of Saul's kingship.

In three brief chapters, Saul's ascent to the throne is complete. He has been called by God, filled with God's spirit, and empowered by God's spirit. It will only take three brief chapters to record Saul's spiral into failure.

After an anti-monarchial speech delivered by Samuel in chapter 12, 1 Samuel 13 records the beginning of Saul's demise. This sudden shift in Samuel's attitude from the end of chapter 12 to the speech in chapter 13 alerts the reader to the impending transition. Samuel will suggest no more celebrations or affirmations. Rather, the downward spiral begins with Samuel's anger in regard to Saul's pre-battle sacrifice. As we previously discussed at length, Saul had become impatient with the deteriorating military situation and the tardiness of Samuel, so he conducted the ritual sacrifice.

The second story in Saul's successive slide is recorded in 1 Samuel 14. Jonathan, Saul's son, initiated military action against the Philistines and eventually won a great battle. In the course of the day, however, Jonathan, faint with hunger, ate honey from a honeycomb he found. After placing the sweet syrup in his mouth, he learned from his troops of an oath his father had made earlier without Jonathan's knowledge. The rash oath cursed anyone who ate on this day of battle.

Jonathan the Brave
(Illustration Credit: Barclay Burns)

Jonathan was not impressed with his father's command, for he knew how hungry and weary the troops were. By the end of the narrative, the oath has twice backfired on Saul. In an attempt to produce holiness with his oath, he prompted unholiness. The troops were so hungry, they slaughtered the animals taken as spoils of war and ravenously devoured the flesh with the blood still in it. Saul also learned that his son had disobeyed his command with regard to the honey. Saul must break his oath or kill his son. Both the consumption of blood and the breaking of the oath were contrary to Levitical law.

The final episode in this spiraling trilogy is Saul's sparing of King Agag of the Amalekites. In 1 Samuel 15:2, the Lord instructs Saul through Samuel to destroy the Amalekites and spare nothing or no one. Saul, however, spares King Agag, as well as the best of the cattle and livestock. Samuel prophesies against Saul at the request of God. God expresses regret (v. 11) and sorrow (v. 35) with regard to his choice of Saul as king. Unlike the well-intentioned sacrifice of chapter 13 and the oath of chapter 14, this merciful sparing of Agag was a direct disobedience of God's command. The chapter ends with a sense of separation. Samuel separates himself from Saul, and the reader senses that God steps away as well.

The first words of chapter 16 are God's instructions to Samuel concerning the anointing of the next king. While Saul will continue to reign in Israel and be written into the story for sixteen more chapters, his tenure as a main character was brief. The literary structure squeezes Saul uncomfortably between Samuel and David. The best days of Israel's faith lie behind him and before him.

These occurrences are indicative of the theological tension in which Saul existed. In each case, it seems Saul's motivations are honest and well-intentioned, even reverent. It is difficult to tell if his actions provoked the justice of God or merely the jealousy of Samuel. But regardless of the source, Saul was in theological turmoil. He was appointed, but he was under the law. He was anointed, but he had to answer to a covenant weighted toward justice. He was chosen but he was chastised. Saul is caught on the bridge between law and grace. Centuries later, a group of exiled Israelites in Babylon would find themselves caught on the same bridge.

1 Samuel 15:33—Samuel had no interest in keeping King Agag alive as a war trophy, as did Saul. Doré's skill as a printmaker can be found in his dramatic use of shading and contrast. The primary action is centered and concentrated on the main protagonists in the narrative.

Gustave Doré (1832–83). *Death of Agag* from the *Illustrated Bible*. 19th century. Engraving. (Credit: Dover Pictoral Archive Series)

TENSIONS IN LIFE

Of Samuel, Saul, and David, the exiled Israelites may have best related to Saul. His record in the biblical text feels the most human. His theological questions and confusions are the fibers that form the common faith experience. The exiled Israelites could see themselves in Saul. Saul was chosen; Israel was chosen.

Saul was subject to the often ambiguous sermons of a prophet; Israel had her prophets as well. Saul tried to find himself somewhere between law and grace; Israel was in the same quandary.

The most basic phrase used to describe God's relationship with Israel in the Old Testament is "people of Yahweh" (*'am YHWH*).[16] Yahweh was the personal name of God revealed to Moses during his call experience. Prior to the exodus, Israel was little more than an extended family. But after the exodus, Israel was a nation whose God was Yahweh. The Exodus record and the subsequent Deuteronomic History both reflect upon how Israel is to live out this unique relationship.

This theme of chosenness is also prevalent in the writings of Deutero-Isaiah. This portion of Isaiah's prophecy (chs. 40–55) was delivered during the Babylonian exile. The prophet offered hope to the captives by consistently reminding them that they were God's chosen (41:8), in whom he delights (42:1), and were created for his purpose (44:2). One can imagine that the Israelites felt as chosen and hopeful in Babylon as Saul did in the presence of Samuel.

Speaking of Isaiah and Samuel, the exiled Israelites struggled with their prophets just as Saul had struggled with his. The pre-exilic prophets had warned of the coming captivity, but in words that left little room for repentance. Though Amos, Micah, Isaiah, and Zephaniah prophesy over a period of decades, their warnings primarily concern what "will" happen and not what "might" happen. Israel's exilic fate seemed set. It was as if God had decided to deliver them into the hands of the Babylonians and then told them they had done wrong, much like Samuel's accusations and judgments in 1 Samuel 13. This argument does not excuse Israel's disobedience; it simply highlights the frustration of prophetic timing as experienced by both Saul and Israel.

The theological tension that emerges from the exilic experience is obvious. The "people of Yahweh" have become the captives of Babylon. The nation that enjoyed God's promise of eternal, steadfast love and mercy has seemingly found a boundary to God's presence. This population that had claimed the grace of the Davidic covenant have found themselves judged by more Mosaic standards. Isaiah, Ezekiel, and other exilic prophets tried to comfort Israel by reminding them of God's steadfast love and mercy. Israel, however, knew that the weight had shifted toward law. The chosen people had become a chastised people who could only hope.

The role of prophets has changed very little today. They stand and speak a word for God. At times it is difficult to distinguish if the word is holy or human in origin; distinguishing between divine piety and human personality can be confusing. At their best, however, the prophets challenge our vested interests in particular covenants. When we rest too securely in the grace of God, they preach to us from the Law of Moses. When we are guilt-ridden over our shortcomings, they remind us of the steadfast love promised to David.

In the process, we learn that God's nature embraces both covenants. God's actions are typically weighted toward one covenant in response to our actions. Our faith must be lived in the theological tension that exists between these covenants—between law and grace.

CONVEYING THE TENSION

Guiding the Worshiper

Synopsis of Worship Theme

Saul's fateful existence within the tension of law and grace is not unique. Every worshiper brings similar internal struggles to the sanctuary. Some carry a weight of guilt and shame that arises from their humanity, seemingly preventing their achievement of holiness. They typically live, unconsciously, within the influence of the Mosaic covenant. Others enter the sanctuary with a twisted confidence in the grace of God. Because they have chosen God (and feel that God has chosen them), their actions take a backseat to the fervency of their belief. They are "sure" they are saved, "certain" they have an eternal home, and they believe Christ's blood covers a multitude of sins. Their often unconscious embrace of Davidic covenant relieves them of giving attention to God's expectations for their lives.

In three movements, the following worship service addresses this spectrum of participants. In the first movement, labeled *Entering the Mysterious Presence of God,* the congregation will affirm through Scripture, song, and prayer that both covenants—aspects of law *and* grace—necessarily exist within the nature of God. The Call to Worship, taken from Exodus 34, is a litany of self-disclosure, spoken by God to Moses, that highlights the tense relationship of law and grace within the heart of God. The hymn and prayer that follow continue this theme.

In the second movement, titled *Adhering to the Law of God,* worshipers will be led to engage God's expectations for their lives and prayerfully confess shortcomings. This will be accomplished through the presentation of the Ten Commandments followed by prayers of confession and assurance.

The final movement, *Embracing the Grace of God*, will be primarily expressed through anthem and sermon. It is here that I must admit my own covenantal bias. While in some churches it may be easier to focus on the legal expectations of God in the life of humanity, I believe that a primary ministry of the church (if not *the* primary ministry of the church) is the offer of grace.

Philip Yancey, a popular Christian author and educator, shared these words from a private conversation with Gordon MacDonald. MacDonald said, "The world can do almost anything as well or better than the church. You need not be a Christian to build houses, feed the hungry, or heal the sick. There is only one thing the world cannot do. It cannot offer grace."[17] In light of this great truth, the worship service will present both stereotypical extremes of the theological tension found in the life of Saul, but its climax and conclusion will be weighted toward grace.

Suggested Order of Worship

ENTERING THE MYSTERIOUS PRESENCE OF GOD
Organ Prelude
Chiming of the Hour
Call to Worship
   Minister: The Lord passed before Moses and proclaimed,
   People: The Lord, The Lord, a God merciful and gracious, slow to anger, and abounding in steadfast love and faithfulness,
   Minister: keeping steadfast love for the thousandeth generation, forgiving iniquity and transgression and sin,
   People: yet by no means clearing the guilty,
   Minister: but visiting the iniquity of the parents upon children and the children's children, to the third and fourth generation.
   All: And Moses quickly bowed his head toward the earth, and worshiped.

Hymn of Praise 6   "Immortal, Invisible, God Only Wise"   ST. DENIO
Invocation
Welcome of Worshipers
   Minister: The Lord be with you.
   People: And also with you.
   Minister: We have gathered in the presence of a God who administers both justice and grace according to divine pleasure.
   People: May God find pleasure in our love of the law and desire for grace this hour.

Adult *The Theological Tension*

ADHERING TO THE LAW OF GOD
Scripture Lesson　　　　　Exodus 20:1-18
Prayer of Confession
Hymn of Assurance 134　　"Jesus Paid It All"　　　　　　　ALL TO CHRIST
Children's Sermon

EMBRACING THE GRACE OF GOD
Hymn of Offering 25　　　"There's a Wideness in God's Mercy"　WELLESLEY
Offertory Prayer
Offertory
The Doxology
Scripture Lesson　　　　　1 Samuel 13:1-14
Pastoral Prayer
Choral Anthem
Message
Hymn of Decision 323　　"Come, Ye Sinners, Poor and Needy"　RESTORATION
Benediction
  Minster: Let us go, living as if salvation depends upon us, and trusting that salvation depends on God.
  People: We will go, with the laws of God and the grace of God written in our hearts.
  All: Amen.

Choral Response
Organ Postlude

Musical Options

Instrumental Music
O Love How Deep, How Broad, How High, David Johnson (organ)
Wondrous Love, Dale Wood (organ)
My Savior's Love, Jusy Swaim (piano)

Anthems
Love Comes from God, Pote, SATB, Hinshaw Music, HMC-1098
God So Loved the World, Stainer, SATB, G. Schirmer, 11717
Lord, Thy Church on Earth Is Seeking, Schweobel, SATB, Genevox, 4171-10

Sermon Outlines

Please note that the following sermon outlines offer you the opportunity to direct your sermon toward either grace or law. The first sermon interprets 1 Samuel 13 with sympathy toward Saul. The preacher is encouraged to compliment the efforts of Saul with regard to the ritual offering and expound upon the necessity of grace that was not given by Samuel. The second sermon interprets 1 Samuel 13 with sympathy toward Samuel. The preacher is encouraged to view the ritual offering of Saul as a failure and expound the necessity of repentance.

Both interpretations may be defended as valid given the literary structure and content of the text. Such is the tension that exists between law and grace.

When Our Best Is Not Enough (An Expository Outline)

In a book titled *Shame and Grace*, Lewis Smedes, a professor of psychology at Fuller Theological seminary, addresses the seemingly universal struggle with shame. He pinpoints three sources from which this burden arises: the secular culture that attempts to define how a person should look and feel; unaccepting parents who convince us we will never live up to their expectations; and religious institutions that instruct us to follow rules explicitly or face eternal punishment.[18] Even at our best, none of us are able to live up to the expectations these arenas of influence place upon us. As humans, our best never seems to be enough. The same was true for Saul.

(1) Saul faced the challenge of the throne. (v. 1)
(2) Saul faced the challenge of military leadership. (vv. 2-4)
(3) Saul faced the challenge of protecting his people. (vv. 5-7)
(4) Saul faced the challenge of patience. (v. 8)
(5) Saul faced the challenge of faith practice. (vv. 9-10)
(6) Saul received the criticism of Samuel. (vv. 11-14)
(7) We must face life assured of God's grace. When Samuel or the church or anyone else critiques our honest, well-intentioned attempts to serve God, we must rely on the assurance of God's grace.

Saul was never given the opportunity to recognize that his reign was merely the first chapter in God's purpose and process for Israel. The expectations placed upon Saul were probably too high. His own self-expectations may have been higher. His life was weighted toward law instead of grace.

Dangerous Curve Ahead (A Narrative Sermon)
Tell the following stories highlighting the successes of each character, but with emphasis on the "turning point" that led to each person's demise.

It seems that from the beginning, God's creatures have been capable of so much good and at the same time, so prone to failure.

(1) Adam and Eve: List successes. Their turning point was a forbidden fruit.
(2) Moses: List successes. His turning point was a rock in the wilderness.
(3) Saul: List successes (three stories in 1 Sam 9–11). His turning point was an altar at Gilgal.
(4) Peter: List successes. His turning point was the accusation of a slave girl.
(5) Us: List successes. Our turning points are one of a hundred ways we fall short of God's glory. We are all in need of repentance and the grace of God through Jesus Christ our Lord.

The grace of God assures us that the "bend in our road" (the negative turning point of life) is not the end of our road with God.

Guiding the Learner

The Occurrence
Serving as the first king of Israel placed Saul in a position of definition. How he served and the roles he played in the life of the nation would set a standard to be followed or adjusted by those who succeeded him. Such is the case with most pioneer efforts.

This realization provides an interesting framework for conveying and discussing the focal text, 1 Samuel 13:1-14. Use the following outline to introduce the passage and discuss Saul's multiple roles in the life of Israel.

(1) Saul the King (v. 1)
(2) Saul the Military Leader (vv. 2-4)
(3) Saul the Pastor (vv. 5-7)
(4) Saul the Priest (vv. 8-10)
(5) Saul the Human (vv. 11-14)

• Were these valid roles for Saul to fill? Why or why not?
• What strengths and weaknesses did he display within each role?

The Memory

As previously stated, Saul may be the character in the Deuteronomic History with whom the exiled Israelites most easily identified. While Samuel seems to do no wrong—and David will do wrong, yet be forgiven—Saul's life is a down-to-earth mix of emotions and decisions for which he is fatefully held responsible. He will accept God's call to be king, he will be chastised for his failure to execute the role properly, and he will eventually reign in the shadow of another who is chosen to replace him. This is a chronology with which Israel can relate. The exiles had been God's chosen people, were being chastised for not executing that role properly, and seemed to exist in the shadow of a foreign government ordained by their God.

The following broad outline of Saul's life will convey to your students a literary structure that accentuates the chronology of his experience: positive ascent, negative demise, and an eventual secondary role in the story of Israel and God.

I. The Positive Ascent of Saul
   A. Saul is chosen by God. (1 Sam 9)
   B. Saul is anointed by God. (1 Sam 10)
   C. Saul is empowered by God. (1 Sam 11)

II. The Demise of Saul
   A. An inappropriate sacrifice at Gilgal (1 Sam 13)
   B. An inappropriate oath in Ephraim (1 Sam 14)
   C. An inappropriate sparing of Agag (1 Sam 15)

III. The Secondary Role of Saul
   A. Saul is comforted by David. (1 Sam 16)
   B. Saul is defended by David. (1 Sam 17)
   C. Saul is jealous of David. (1 Sam 18–20)
   D. Saul pursues David. (1 Sam 21–26)
   E. Saul's death grieves David. (1 Sam 31)

It is painfully obvious that the appearances of Saul after David's anointing in 1 Samuel 16 are for the purpose of moving David's story. Saul has become a secondary character.

The Interpretation

The following readings are suggested to help your students engage the theological tension that exists between law and grace. The first reading addresses the tension as it exists within the nature of God, the second as it exists within the nature of humanity, and the third as it exists within the nature of the church.

Reading #1—Exodus 34:6-8

Reading #2—A college professor attempted to resolve the tension between law and grace by telling his class, "We must work as if salvation completely depends upon us, but trust that salvation completely depends upon God."

Reading #3—Recently I have been asking a question of strangers—for example, seatmates on an airplane—when I strike up a conversation. "When I say the words 'evangelical Christian' what comes to mind?" In reply, mostly I hear political descriptions: of strident pro-life activists, or gay-rights opponents, or proposals for censoring the Internet . . . Not once—*not once*—have I heard a description redolent of grace. Apparently that is not the aroma Christians give off in the world.[19]

- Does it surprise you that theological tension exists in the life of God? Humanity? The church? Why or why not?
- What contradictions and struggles do the above readings present?
- How have you experienced these tensions, struggles, and contradictions in your life? As a parent? As a child? As an employee? As a church member?
- Is your life weighted toward law or grace? The life of your family? Your friends? Your church?
- Why is the balance between law and grace so important?

NOTES

[1] Walter Brueggemann, *Theology of the Old Testament* (Minneapolis: Fortress Press, 1997), 419.

[2] Brevard S. Childs, *Introduction to the Old Testament as Scripture* (Philadelphia: Fortress Press, 1979), 277.

[3] Eugene H. Peterson, *First and Second Samuel* (Louisville: Westminster John Knox Press, 1999), 75.

4 Ralph W. Klein, *I Samuel*, Word Biblical Commentary (Waco: Word, Incorporated, 1993), 124.

5 Tony W. Cartledge, *I & II Samuel*, Smyth & Helwys Bible Commentary (Macon: Smyth and Helwys Publishing, Inc., 2001), 172.

6 Peterson, 79.

7 Cartledge, 174.

8 Walter Brueggemann, *First and Second Samuel*, Interpretation, A Bible Commentary for Teaching and Preaching (Louisville: John Knox Press, 1990), 99.

9 Peterson, 79.

10 John Claypool, *Glad Reunion, Meeting Ourselves in the Lives of Bible Men and Women* (Waco: Word Incorporated, 1985), 85.

11 R. P. Gordon, *1 & 2 Samuel* (Sheffield England: Sheffield Academic Press, 1984), 55.

12 Brueggemann, *Samuel*, 100.

13 Ibid., 102.

14 Ibid., 101.

15 Bruce C. Birch, Walter Brueggemann, Terrence E. Fretheim, David L. Petersen, *A Theological Introduction to the Old Testament* (Nashville: Abingdon Press, 1999), 230.

16 Brevard S. Childs, *Biblical Theology of the Old and New Testaments, Theological Reflection on the Christian Bible* (Minneapolis: Fortress Press, 1992), 421.

17 Philip Yancey, *What's So Amazing about Grace?* (Grand Rapids: Zondervan Publishing House, 1997), 15.

18 Lewis B. Smedes, *Shame and Grace* (San Francisco: Harper-Collins, 1993), 80.

19 Yancey, 31.

Chapter Four

THE RELATIONAL TENSION

DAVID: WEAK BUT WINNING

Focal Text: 1 Samuel 16:1-13   Broader Text: 1 Samuel 16–2 Samuel 24

I endured the torture many times during my childhood. My small frame, short stature, and late growth spurt (I'm still waiting on the growth spurt) left me vulnerable to the strengths of other children my age. As is common on most playgrounds and in most backyards, we would gather for a game of football or softball. Captains would be appointed and the choosing of teams would begin. My only hope of being chosen anywhere but last was if Kenneth Baxter, my best friend, was a captain. Even then, there were days when he couldn't sacrifice the win for my weakness.

We live in a competitive world. Regardless of our daily contexts, we contend with situations and individuals that expose our weaknesses. At times they can be concealed; at other times they are quite conspicuous. Once revealed, they often become the basis of our being chosen for particular tasks . . . or overlooked. Orchestras hold try-outs to assess acceptance and determine seatings. Law students must pass the bar, PhD candidates undergo oral exams, and potential physicians endure the boards in order to assure the world they are capable and worthy of being chosen. I've known people aspiring to each of these fields. They have feared, yes *feared*, the process of testing because deep within us, we know our weaknesses. Our weaknesses have the potential to keep us from being chosen; they keep us from winning.

The people of God were exiled in Babylon for more than fifty years. They were weak. It appeared God had chosen Babylon ahead of them. They needed a hero to remind them that God is not beyond choosing the weak and making them winners. That hero emerged from their memories in the person of a king named David.

TENSIONS IN THEOLOGY

As stated in the previous chapter, Saul was perhaps the one character in the Deuteronomic record with whom Israel (and perhaps humanity) could most easily identify. David, however, is the most popular and familiar character of 1 and 2 Samuel. This is not because we so easily identify with David, but rather because we would *like* to identify with him. David is a hero. David is the quintessential underdog who is able to overcome. David is weak, but he wins. He is who we wish to be and who the exiles longed to be.

David survived what is perhaps one of the most common sources of tension—human relationships. While individuals have been a part of the tensions we have previously observed in 1 and 2 Samuel, these tensions typically emerged from circumstances larger than the individuals involved. Political tensions existed between competing systems. Theological tensions existed between competing doctrines and ideals. The relational tensions of the Davidic saga will exist between individuals—the weak and the strong.

Weakness is always relative. A person is only weak in comparison to one who is stronger. If an individual existed alone, the idea of weak and strong would not exist. It is because we are relational creatures that the idea of competitive weakness and strength subsist. This is a relational tension.

The "selection process" heightens this tension further, however. If the strong were always chosen and always won, the tension would be minimal. Pecking orders would be established and our primary tension would be internal. We would wish to be stronger, struggle to be stronger, maybe even despise those who were stronger. But only those who found themselves relatively weak would experience this type of tension. The introduction of a selection process, however, opens new possibilities; new possibilities heighten the tension.

As a child on the school playground, it was possible for me to be chosen first even though I was weakest. I had a friend. Sometimes relationship took precedence over strength. And who knows, maybe after my selection, we could gain some really strong players and win. Or maybe I'm chosen last, but chosen by a strong team that wins. Or maybe, by some twist of fate, we execute the perfect play at the perfect time and win. Or maybe the other team makes a fatal error allowing us to win. The possibilities are endless within a relational system that depends upon a selection process. It is possible to be weak and still win. This creates tension, not only for the weak, but also for those with power.

With God, all things are possible—the possibilities are endless. To be chosen by God places even the weakest individuals in a position to win. It also places the powerful in a vulnerable situation; relational tension is created. This mysterious, unpredictable God of Israel often operates as a friend. Like a Kenneth Baxter of the cosmos, God will often choose the weaker on the basis of relationship rather than inherent strength. God will choose those whose hearts are well developed rather than their muscles or even their minds. In fact, this unpredictable God almost predictably chooses the unexpected, weaker individuals to carry the ball.

Maybe it began with the forming of humankind from the dust of the earth and then giving humanity responsibility for the earth from which they came. We certainly see God's predictably unpredictable pattern of choice continued in the selection of Jacob the younger over Esau the older. God chooses Joseph, the younger, instead of ten older siblings. God chooses Moses, a murderous stuttering fugitive, rather than one of hundreds of other candidates for bringing about deliverance. God puts Rahab the harlot on his team. And among the judges of Israel, Deborah, a woman, is listed.

Within 1 and 2 Samuel, the pattern has continued. Eli expected his sons to serve as judges over Israel, but God chose a little boy named Samuel. Samuel expected his sons to serve as judges over Israel, but God chose Saul, a self described "Benjamite, from the least of the tribes of Israel, and my family is the humblest of all the families of the tribe" (1 Sam 9:21). And then there is David.

For the exiled children of Israel, the stories of David provided a source of hope. The Jews were relatively weak in comparison to the Babylonians. But if God could use the youngest of brothers, a singing shepherd boy, to kill giants, then there was hope. These Davidic stories of faith served to undergird Israel's hope that the biggest and strongest and best and first do not always win. It is simply the one God chooses for God's own reasons and God's own purposes. Maybe God would choose Israel again.

TENSIONS IN TEXT

David. The mere mention of his name conjures images that are larger than life. There are few individuals in Israel's history who have grown to the biblical proportions of this monarchial mammoth. His mythic popularity has invaded the culture and fabric of almost every generation. Michelangelo carved him in stone. He was portrayed in film by Richard Gere. He has been embraced by almost every child in the Jewish and Christian traditions as the ultimate hero of Bible storybooks.

The Davidic saga dominates the pages of 1 and 2 Samuel and perhaps, outside of Moses, the complete pages of Hebrew Scripture. Within 1 and 2 Samuel, the Davidic narratives cover forty of the fifty-five chapters of these two books. Hints of Davidic royalty occur as early as the Song of Hannah in 1 Samuel 2:10. Every other character in 1 and 2 Samuel, including Samuel and Saul, appear to exist in order to move the larger story toward David. It is no literary accident that in chapters 16–24 of 1 Samuel, all three primary characters are active, but David is obviously dominant.

David is a literary character who stretches beyond the boundaries of 1 and 2 Samuel. In the Book of Kings, the Deuteronomic continuation of Israel's history, "King David" are the first words of the Hebrew text. His recorded death and subsequent influence set the stage for the record of Solomon's reign in this portion of Scripture.

A later historian, the Chronicler, also retells David's story (in 1 Chronicles). By this point in Israel's history (4th or 5th century BC), David has been further idealized. The Chronicler, unlike the earlier Deuteronomic Historian, deletes the story of David's adultery with Bathsheba, as well as other murky details, from the king's record. Rather, he tends to focus exclusively on David's triumphs and able leadership.[1]

Although David's scope and influence permeates much of biblical text, we can best understand the relational tensions of his life by first surveying his humble beginnings. In 1 Samuel 16, the choosing and anointing of David is recorded. The relational tension between weakness and power are immediately evident. In vv. 1-2, God instructs Samuel to prepare to anoint the next king of Israel. The tension is obvious. Saul is still alive and Samuel is overwhelmed with the mixed emotions of grief and fear. The royal power that Samuel first anointed has failed—grief. That same power will not be pleased with the anointing of a new king—fear. It is ironic that this fiery prophet and priest has come to fear the king he once so easily confronted and condemned. God may have chosen Samuel for this task not just to accomplish a work in David's life, but also to reassure Samuel during an internal struggle with personal perceived weakness. Even God's use of a lie to protect Samuel from Saul is indicative of the weakness of Saul's thinking as opposed to Samuel's. After all, who would believe such a powerful prophet would travel to such a small village to offer a sacrifice?

This small village of Bethlehem presents a less obvious, but very important, expression of relational tension. This is the town from which the new king will

> **David's Résumé**
>
>
>
> King David Playing the Lute. Relief from Pueto de las platerias. Romanesque. 12th century. Santiago de Compostela, Spain. (Credit: Giraudon/Art Resource)
>
> David's initial qualification was his skill with the lyre, literally, "He knows harp-playing." Two unexpected epithets follow: "Man of valor" translates *gibbôr ḥayil*, an appellative that can emphasize physical prowess, financial power, or family stature. "Warrior" means, literally, "a man of war." Both of these titles seem overblown when describing a shepherd boy! David's intelligence and poise are conveyed by the phrase "prudent in speech," for the word rendered "prudent" means "insightful," "discerning," or "intelligent."
>
> David not only was intelligent and skilled, but also he was handsome and fit, described as "a man of good presence." The word "presence" literally means "form" or "outline." David was physically fit and attractive.
>
>
>
> Andrea del Verocchio (1435–88). *David.* c. 1470. Bronze. 49⅝" Museo Nazionale del Bargello. Florence, Italy. (Credit: Scala/Art Resource)
>
> David's final attribute is his best one: "Yahweh is with him." What Saul did not realize is that it was the spirit of Yahweh in David that would give him comfort, not simply his music.

be chosen. In v. 2, Samuel is told to go "to Jesse the Bethlehemite, for I have provided for myself a king among his sons." Bethlehem was outside the governed territories of Saul and it was not a part of the usual Ramah-Bethel-Mizpah route of Samuel's influence.[2] This was new territory outside the established power structures of Israel. It was a weak place that secretly held the anointed of God—a heritage which would continue until the realization of the Christian Messiah.

Although Samuel's "sacrificial excuse" for traveling to Bethlehem was apparently adequate enough to distract Saul's anger, it was not solid enough to diminish the elders' fear. In v. 4, the elders of the town "came to meet [Samuel] trembling," and they questioned his intentions. The elders of the town were typically the oldest and wisest the families of the town had to offer. They would meet at the city gate to settle disputes, enforce laws, and serve as witness to business transactions.[3] They recognized Samuel and immediately became suspicious of his presence. Even with the local governing power they enjoyed, they felt weak in Samuel's presence. Weakness is always relative. Samuel shares the "sacrificial excuse" with them, but the reader senses they do not buy it. It was in 1 Samuel 8:4 that the "elders" of Israel asked for a king. And the last time they saw Samuel with a "horn of oil" was at the anointing of Saul. Samuel is carrying the horn again.

Verses 6-12 contain the literary climax toward which these smaller vignettes of relational tension have been moving. The sons of Jesse are paraded before Samuel. It appears that only Samuel knows the purpose of this pageant and only Samuel hears the urgings of God. In v. 6, Eliab, the oldest son of Jesse, passes before Samuel. Samuel is enamoured with his apparent strength and stature. But God advises Samuel against this visual method of selection in v. 7. God's mention of appearance and height as inadequate qualifications for royalty prompts the reader to remember the description of Saul in 1 Samuel 10:23: "[Saul] was head and shoulders taller than any of them."

Six more sons pass before Samuel in vv. 8-10, but none are chosen. Samuel, quite sure of his mission and obviously baffled at the silence of God, finally asks, "Are all your sons here?" Jesse's response contains the pivotal word for relational tension, "There remains yet the youngest, but..." *But.* In the mind of Jesse, in the mind of Eliab, in the mind of Abinadab, and probably in the minds of everyone else in the house, the one remaining child was the least expected to be chosen. But on the playground of faith, this child has caught the eye of God. And so we wait to meet the unlikely candidate for king.

There is no reference to how long they waited, but it must have taken a while. The child was outside the house. He was somewhere tending the sheep. Within this book that relies on tension, the Deuteronomic Historian does a wonderful job in v. 11 of making everyone wait: Jesse's family, Samuel, the reader, and all of Israel.[4] We are all waiting for the eighth son. Seven, the typically perfect number, have passed. We are waiting on the eighth—a number in Hebrew literature that often signifies something new is about to happen.

Finally, he enters. Although we have been informed that appearance matters little, the first words out of the narrator's pen are compliments concerning the boy's physical appearance. His skin, his eyes, and his persona were too striking to ignore. God immediately instructs Samuel to anoint David, "for this is the one" (1 Sam 16:12).

In v. 13, Samuel anoints David with oil, the symbolic expression of God's blessing. But the text also says that God's spirit came mightily upon him "from that day forward." The spirit of God had empowered Saul, but it was not directly related to his anointing. Nor did the spirit come upon Saul with a sense of permanence. David's reception of God's spirit was directly tied to the anointing and the text implies a sense of permanence.[5]

It is during the report of David's reception of God's spirit that we see his name in text for the first time. This Cinderella Story of the eleventh century BC has finally been introduced to the world. The one they never assumed would be king has been anointed. The children who were usually picked first on the playground were overlooked. David was weak... but winning.

1 Samuel 16—Carolsfeld has captured Jesse's surprise at learning that God had chosen David, rather than one of his older sons, to be king.

Julius Schnoor von Carolsfeld. *David Is Anointed King.* 19th century. Woodcut. *Das Buch der Bucher in Bilden.* (Credit: Dover Pictorial Archive Series)

As we watch the Davidic story move beyond our focal text, it is easy to observe the continued development of the aforementioned relational tension. The difficulty, however, is finding a way to cover the breadth of this amazing saga. The books of 1 and 2 Samuel were originally one book. Their division in the Protestant Bible denotes one way the saga can be understood. The break between 1 and 2 Samuel correlates with the death of Saul. David's story is then separated—David before the death of Saul and David after the death of Saul.

Others have used 2 Samuel 11 as a mark of division in the Davidic saga. Second Samuel 11 records the story of David's adulterous relationship with Bathsheba and the negative consequences that followed. In light of this pivotal moment, some scholars label 1 Samuel 16 the beginning of "The History of David's Rise" and 2 Samuel 10 the beginning of the "The History of David's Fall."[6] This idea of ascending and descending is a bit overstated, however. Even though it appears David's life takes a downward turn in the later chapters of 2 Samuel, some of his most profound spiritual moments will occur during these periods of difficulty and visible weakness.[7]

Rather than look at the broader narrative of David's life with an eye toward its chronological relationship to Saul or its ethical ebb in relationship to Bathsheba, let's allow it naturally to meander and fluctuate amid the inevitable weak moments of humanness. At times, the saga will expose David's struggles with his own weaknesses. At other times, it will allow us to observe David's response to the weaknesses of others. Remember, weakness is relative. David's ability to exercise vulnerability and empathy made him a king to be remembered.

From the beginning, we have been aware of elements of weakness within David. First Samuel 16–17 paints the earliest portraits of David: a shepherd boy, a young musician, and an unknown warrior. The images convey no inherent power, yet young David always seems to win in spite of himself. The shepherd boy who was treated as a virtual nonentity in the family of Jesse is anointed king.[8] The young musician is able to soothe a reigning king. And the unknown warrior wreaks havoc with the Philistines and their prized giant. David always manages to win. But he is, in these earliest chapters, a marginal character who is uncredentialed and has no real social status.[9]

As we move through the chapters of David's life, we quickly see that some of his weaknesses have nothing to do with credentials or social status, however. As with most of us, many of David's weaknesses are a result of choice and circumstance. His youthful successes created a deep jealousy within the heart of King Saul. This circumstance leads to a period of weakness in the life of David. In 1 Samuel 18–20, David must be protected by Jonathan, the son of Saul. In chapters 21–22, David is harbored and protected by the priests of Nob who eventually give their lives for the fugitive future king. In chapters 27–28, David finds himself ironically sheltered by the Philistines, his former enemies. Like a cat, with at least nine lives, David continually lands on his feet. He does what he must to survive.

The next extended episode of David's weaknesses begins in 2 Samuel 11. David chooses to commit adultery with Bathsheba and plots the death of her husband Uriah. The prophet Nathan parabolicly confronts David and David unknowingly pronounces his own judgment—death (2 Sam 12). Nathan informs David that "the LORD has put away your sin; you shall not die." But death is the verdict for the firstborn son of David and Bathsheba. And following that death, violence never seems to leave the house of David.

Second Samuel 13–20 is a painful succession of weak moments in the life of David and his family. Amnon, David's son, rapes his half-sister Tamar. Absalom, Tamar's brother, kills Amnon in revenge. Though Absalom is later restored to the family after a period of banishment, bitterness and hatred have infiltrated the family system. Eventually Absalom leads a revolt against David. When the rebellion ends, Absalom is dead at the hands of Joab, David's trusted general. A grief-stricken David is barely able to keep his mind on the affairs of the kingdom in chapter 19. But before this painful series of events ends, David has to muster the strength to squash a revolt by Sheba, the son of Bichri, in chapter 20. The weakened king continues to find a way to survive... and win.

The Davidic saga not only exposes the weaknesses within David, but it vividly displays his empathy for the weak. It is a part of David's magnetism to attract the political and economic outcasts of Israel.[10] In 1 Samuel 18, David forges a deep friendship with Jonathan, Saul's son. Although it seems at times that Jonathan protects David, David is also keenly aware of the weak moment Jonathan endures. Jonathan is the king's son, but he will not inherit the throne. David affords a unique friendship to the politically lame young man.

This illustration imagines that David was playing the harp, rather than napping, prior to his encounter with Bathsheba.

Julius Schnoor von Carolsfeld. *David and Bathsheba*. 19th century. Woodcut. *Das Buch der Bucher in Bilden*. (Credit: Dover Pictorial Archive Series)

Even while David lives the life of a fugitive, he is sensitive to the needs of those who are weak. In 1 Samuel 22, David hides from Saul in the cave of Adullam. Word of his whereabouts spread quickly through the impoverished corners of Saul's kingdom, and 22:2 records, "Everyone who was in distress, and everyone who was in debt, and everyone who was discontented gathered to him." In 1 Samuel 25, this wandering group of vagabonds approaches the property of Nabal and his wife Abigail. Nabal was "surly and mean" and refused to aid David and his entourage. The small army was about to attack the home of Nabal, when Abigail brought gifts and begged for her family's safety. David was swayed by her humble plea and granted this weak woman's request. (Ten days later, the Lord struck Nabal dead.)

David's care for those who are weak extended to Saul's family after his death (2 Sam 9) and to the complete Israelite family during times of famine (2 Sam 21). David knew pain and seemed ready to address the pain in others.

Probably the most unique aspect of David's empathy, however, was his ability to patiently understand, or at least tolerate, the weaknesses that existed in the hearts of the powerful. It cannot be overlooked that David never relinquished his loyalty to and affection for Saul. Twice David had opportunity to kill Saul, yet he spared him (1 Sam 24 and 26). And at Saul's death, David and all the men who were with him "mourned and wept, and fasted until evening." This same reaction occurred at the deaths of Abner and Eshbaal. David conducted himself impeccably as he awaited the throne.[11] He understood and endured the weaknesses that exist in people of power. David realized that the "up and in" need God's grace just as desperately as the "down and out." This weak and wonderful hero had much to convey to a nation in Babylonian exile.

TENSIONS IN LIFE

In the early chapters of David's life it seems he can do no wrong. In the later chapters of David's life, the imperfections begin to show, but the celebrated king of Israel always manages to maintain favor. He is favored by the people. First Samuel 18 reiterates this trait five times: v. 1, Jonathan loved him; v. 3, Jonathan loved him; v. 16, all Israel and Judah loved him; v. 20, Michal loved him; and v. 28 Michal and/or all Israel loved him.[12] He was favored by God. Numerous times the narrator reminds us, "the LORD was with (David)" (1 Sam 17:37; 18:12, 14, 28; 20:13; 2 Sam 5:10). God's presence and providence were allied with David in spite of his weaknesses. There is no doubt that David represented Israel's future in the mind of God.[13]

David was a survivor. As a vulnerable young warrior, he survived. As a fugitive, in the cross hairs of Saul, in the hands of priests, and even in the camp of the Philistines, he survived. He survived the death of a child as well as the rebellion and death of another child. He survived war and famine and grief. He just found a way to survive and to help others survive.

It is no wonder the story of David dominates the Deuteronomic Historian's words for the exiled Israelites in Babylon. It is no wonder that King David emerged as a hero for captive children and adults alike. It is no surprise that this is the character the exiles would most like to resemble. The exiles need to know they are loved. The exiles need to know that even in their weakest moments, God's presence and providence are still on their side. The exiles, who have already framed their experience as punishment, need to be reminded of the steadfast love and favor promised to David. The exiles need just enough hope to survive . . . and to help others survive.

There is always a relational aspect to weakness. For one to know weakness, there must be a strong entity. David reminds us that we are all relatively weak. We have all made choices that exposed our internal weaknesses. We have all endured circumstances that pitted us against family members, coworkers,

Adult   *The Relational Tension*

authorities, and friends. We have all faced the giants of loneliness, loss, fatigue, insecurity, and grief. We have all prayed to survive.

And if we have been fortunate enough to remain relatively strong in comparison to the world around us, then the world around us is experiencing the weakness. As people of God, our sensitivities are heightened to those who hurt. Being honestly aware of our own weaknesses helps us recognize the weaknesses with which others struggle. Being joyfully thankful that we have survived, we can offer others hope for survival.

The Apostle Paul spent much of his Christian life enduring the pains associated with his faith. He was physically assaulted, verbally assaulted, and imprisoned on numerous occasions. But this Hebrew of Hebrews, from the small tribe of Benjamin, was told by God, "my power is made perfect in weakness" (2 Cor 12:9). And toward the end of his life, the Apostle shared these words with the Roman Christians:

> Who will separate us from the love of Christ? Will hardship, or distress, or persecution, or famine, or nakedness, or peril, or the sword?... No, in all these things we are more than conquerors though him who loves us. For I am convinced that neither death, nor life, nor angels, nor rulers, nor things present, nor things to come, nor powers, nor height, nor depth, nor anything else in all creation will be able to separate us from the love of God in Christ Jesus our Lord.

We will survive. The weak will win.

CONVEYING THE TENSION

Guiding the Worshiper

Synopsis of Worship Theme

During the course of this worship service, the participant will hear several stories from the life of David. These stories serve as "introductory words" for particular elements of worship. The gathering of the distressed in the Cave of Adullam (1 Sam 22) corresponds to the gathering of the people for worship. David's adulterous relationship with Bathsheba (2 Sam 11) ushers the worshiper toward a time of confession. David's inability to defeat the giant, Ishbibenob, without the help of his friends (2 Sam 21:15-17) naturally leads to a time of intercession. And David's musical affirmation of God's goodness in 2 Samuel 22 sets the stage for a time of offering.

The Davidic saga is rich and deep. You may choose other stories to serve as transitions in the service. This service assumes, however, that the depth and diversity of the stories are adequate for guiding worshipers to recognize their own weaknesses, as well as to be sensitive to the weaknesses and needs of others.

Suggested Order of Worship

GOD'S PEOPLE GATHER

Organ Prelude
Chiming of the Hour
Scripture Lesson 1 Samuel 22:1-2
Hymn of Gathering 323 "Come, Ye Sinners, Poor and Needy" RESTORATION
Invocation
Welcome of Worshipers

Minister: The Lord be with you.

People: And also with you.

Minister: This is a house of prayer for all people. Christ welcomes you here.

People: We welcome the presence of Christ in our midst.

GOD'S PEOPLE CONFESS

Scripture Lesson 2 Samuel 11:1-17
Silent Prayers of Confession
The Church Confesses

Minister: Let us confess our sins to God.

All: Almighty God, our heavenly father: We have sinned against you, through our own fault, in thought, and word, and deed, and in what we have left undone. For the sake of your Son our Lord Jesus Christ, forgive us all our offenses; and grant that we may serve you in newness of life, to the glory of your name. Amen.[14]

Minister: Your sins are forgiven.

People: Your sins are forgiven.

Choral Response "Forgiven" RIDGECREST

GOD'S PEOPLE INTERCEDE

Scripture Lesson 2 Samuel 21:15-17
Hymn of Intercession 387 "Blest Be the Tie" DENNIS
Pastoral Prayer

GOD'S PEOPLE GIVE

Scripture Lesson	2 Samuel 22:21-25	
Hymn of Offering 605	"Because I Have Been Given Much"	SEMINARY
Offertory Prayer		
Offertory		
The Doxology		

GOD'S PEOPLE LISTEN

Scripture Lesson	1 Samuel 16:1-13	
Choral Anthem		
Message		
Hymn of Decision 277	"Take My Life, and Let It Be Consecrated"	HENDON
Benediction		
Choral Response		
Organ Postlude		

Musical Options

Instrumental Music
   He Who Will Suffer God to Guide Him, Bach (organ)
   O God Our Help, Paul Manz (organ)
   When We Walk with the Lord, Ovid Young (piano)

Choral Music
   Abide with Me, arr. Martin, SATB, Hinshaw Music, HMC-493
   Be Still My Soul, Courtney, SATB, Breckenhorst Press, BP-1508
   God Is Our Refuge, Pote, SATB, Hope Publishing Co., A583

Sermon Outlines

Power Assessments: 1 Samuel 16:1-13 (An Expository Sermon)
In the family movie *Hook*, Dustin Hoffman plays Captain Hook, the villainous rival of the grown-up Peter Pan, played by Robin Williams. Captain Hook sees himself as a debonair and ageless icon. The Lost Boys see him as a pirate to be feared or fought. His fellow pirates see him as a role model to be emulated. Peter Pan sees him as a providentially defeated adversary. The child heroine of the move sees him as "a mean old man who needs a mommy."

Weakness is always relative. We define our strengths and weaknesses by the perceived strengths and weaknesses of those with whom we are in contact.

I. Sometimes we assume too much power. (1 Sam 16:1-10)
   A. The power of those who govern (vv. 1-3)
   B. The power of those who prophecy (vv. 2-5) (Note that the elders fear the "strong" Samuel, but it was Samuel who first expressed fear of Saul.)
   C. The power of those with "stature" (vv. 6-10)
      1. Physical stature
      2. Social stature (the firstborn)

II. Sometimes we assume too much weakness. (1 Sam 16:11-12)

III. We must always remember the source of true power. (1 Sam 16:13)

A Roller Coaster Ride with God: 1 Samuel 16:1-13 (A Narrative Sermon)
The following stories have been selected to illustrate the ups and downs of David's life. This roller coaster effect should be verbally exaggerated during the sermon. You should feel free to choose other stories from the life of David to create this effect. No doubt, worshipers will relate to the ebb and flow of strength and weakness that is displayed. Most of our lives follow this pattern.

I. Like the first hill on the amusement park roller coaster, David begins the ride of his life with a slow deliberate ascent.
   A. David is anointed king. (1 Sam 16:1-13)
   B. David serves in Saul's court. (1 Sam 16:14-23)
   C. David kills a giant. (1 Sam 17)

II. No sooner is he at the top, in the king's palace and at the king's table, than he begins a hard, fast descent.
   A. David is assaulted by Saul. (1 Sam 18:1-11)
   B. David is pursued by Saul. (1 Sam 19–30)
   C. David grieves for Saul and Jonathan. (2 Sam 1)

III. David is soon climbing again.
   A. David is anointed king of Judah. (2 Sam 2)
   B. David receives the covenant blessing of God. (2 Sam 7)

IV. But he comes crashing down again.
   A. David chooses to commit adultery and murder. (2 Sam 11)
   B. David's family is in turmoil. (2 Sam 13–17)
   C. David loses a son. (2 Sam 18)

V. When David's death is near, he affirms what most of us affirm as we step off the roller coaster of life—God was with me through it all. See David's song (2 Sam 22).

Guiding the Learner

The Occurrence
To convey to your class the relative nature of weakness and strength, present the following outline of the focal passage, 1 Samuel 16:1-13.

I. The perceived strength and real weakness of Saul (vv. 1-3)
II. The perceived strength and real weakness of Samuel (vv. 2-5)
III. The perceived strength and real weakness of Jesse's sons (vv. 6-10)
IV. The perceived weakness and real strength of David (vv. 11-12)
V. The source of all real strength (v. 13)

   Lead the class participants to discuss the strengths and weaknesses that are both presented and implied in the text.
   In order to acquaint your class with the broader strokes of David's "relational portrait" in 1 and 2 Samuel, you may wish to share the following outline.[15]

I. Samuel and David (1 Sam 16)
II. King Saul and Young David (1 Sam 17–18)
III. King Saul and David the Fugitive (1 Sam 19–26)
IV. King Saul and David Separately (1 Sam 27–31)
V. David and Saul's Family (2 Sam 1–5:5)
VI. David Alone (2 Sam 5:6–9:13)
VII. David and His Family (2 Sam 10–20)
VIII. David, his mighty men, and his enemies (2 Sam 21–24)

The Memory
The best and worst times of David's life spoke volumes to the exiled Israelites who remembered his stories. Have individuals or groups within your class read the following narratives from the menagerie of Davidic memories. Ask readers to share a brief synopsis of their assigned text. Then, lead them in discussing the questions listed with regard to each story.

1 Samuel 16:1-13
1 Samuel 17:31-49
1 Samuel 18:1-12
1 Samuel 24:1-17
2 Samuel 7:12-17
2 Samuel 21:15-17

- What strengths and weaknesses are evident in each text?
- What is God's role in each text?
- Where would exiles see themselves in each of these texts?
- How would these stories foster hope in the heart of an exile?

The Interpretation
- Ask class participants to share testimonies of the "up and down" times of their lives. Have them highlight moments of strength and weakness.
- Provide hymnals for class participants and ask them to locate hymns that encourage them in moments of weakness. How are our hymns similar to the Davidic stories?
- Ask participants to identify those whom they consider "weak." How can we, in our relative strength, be more sensitive and serving with regard to their needs?

NOTES

[1] Brevard S. Childs, *Biblical Theology of the Old and New Testaments: Theological Reflection on the Christian Bible* (Minneapolis: Fortress Press, 1992), 154.

[2] Walter Brueggemann, *First and Second Samuel*, Interpretation, A Bible Commentary for Teaching and Preaching (Louisville: John Knox Press, 1990), 120.

[3] Tony W. Cartledge, *I & II Samuel,* Smyth & Helwys Bible Commentary (Macon: Smyth & Helwys Publishing, Inc., 2001), 201.

[4] Brueggeman, *Samuel*, 122.

[5] Ralph W. Klein, *I Samuel*, Word Biblical Commentary (Waco: Word, Incorporated, 1983), 162.

[6] Cartledge, 199.

[7] Brevard S. Childs, *Introduction to the Old Testament as Scripture* (Philadelphia: Fortress Press, 1979), 279.

[8] Eugene H. Peterson, *First and Second Samuel*, (Louisville: Westminster John Knox Press, 1999), 94.

[9] Brueggemann, *Samuel*, 124.

[10] Bruce C. Birch, Walter Brueggemann, Terrence E. Fretheim, David L. Petersen, *A Theological Introduction to the Old Testament* (Nashville: Abingdon Press, 1999), 236.

[11] R. P. Gordon, *I & II Samuel* (Sheffield England: Sheffield Academic Press, 1994), 63.

[12] Walter Brueggemann, *Power, Providence & Personality* (Louisville: Westminster/John Knox Press, 1990), 35.

[13] Birch et al., 236.

[14] *The Book of Common Prayer* (New York: Oxford University Press, 1979), 127.

[15] Carol Stuart Grizzard, "First and Second Samuel," *Mercer Commentary on the Bible* (Macon: Mercer University Press, 1995), 271, 287.

Chapter Five

THE SPIRITUAL TENSION

GOD: COMMITTED BUT NOT CONTROLLED

Focal Text: 2 Samuel 24   Broader Text: 1 and 2 Samuel

Our study of 1 and 2 Samuel has been built around three primary characters: Samuel, Saul, and David. It would have been possible to view this era of Israel's history through the eyes of any series of characters from the books. We could have chosen to orient text, theology, and exilic experience around a series of relatively obscure characters such as Abner, Joab, and Nabal. Or we might have chosen to experience these stories of faith through the eyes of particular women such as Hannah, Abigail, and Michal.

   Regardless of the series of characters chosen to provide a basis for the study of 1 and 2 Samuel, one character must be included in any list and receive our attention . . . God. In this final chapter, we will explore and discuss God's role in the Deuteronomic Historian's record of the beginning of Israel's monarchy. After all, the story is primarily about God. The lives of kings and prophets merely orbit the greater mass of God's promises, judgments, words, will, and sovereignty.[1] It is, in fact, the presence and perceived absence of God in these books that leads to our final tension—the spiritual tension.

TENSION IN THEOLOGY

Too often, we read Scripture with little regard for the intricate role of God in the text. We assume God is behind every scene, directing every character's movement, and consistently, though not visibly, present. These assumptions, however, distract us from the rich detail of God's activity and inactivity. They also cause us to overlook, or at least undervalue, the biblical characters' doubts concerning God's presence and role. We assume God is there. This inclines us to take less seriously God's absence as perceived and expressed by the biblical characters and implied by the biblical narrators.

The perceived presence and absence of God is the source of spiritual tension in 1 and 2 Samuel. We are careful to call this a "perceived" sense of God's presence because we are not trying to make a statement concerning the ontological reality of God's presence. We are simply observing how biblical characters "feel" about God's presence. The sense of God's presence, in the arena of spiritual tension, is completely subjective.

The tension is produced not only by the perception of presence and absence, but also through the issues of commitment and control. When God is present, Israel knows for certain that God is committed. God's presence cannot be controlled, however. As we will see, Israel cannot simply carry the ark of the covenant into battle and be assured of God's presence. They cannot ceremonially perform ritual sacrifice and mandate the presence of God. God will not be manipulated.

Our focal text lies in the division of 2 Samuel that some have called "The Samuel Appendix."[2] Chapters 21–24 appear to be a miscellaneous collection of stories from different periods in David's reign that have been compiled and attached to the end of the book. When I think of an appendix, my mind immediately moves toward the physiological image of an unnecessary appendage, which when infected causes pain in one's right side (or is it the left side?). But since it has no particular function, it can be easily removed from the human body and never missed. This physiological image is only partially applicable to 2 Samuel 24.

It is a painful text. God is angry. God incites sin. And God punishes. It is far from unnecessary, however. This is not a story randomly attached to the end of the book because the narrator couldn't find a better place for it. This is the final chapter. Samuel's story has been told. Saul's story has been told. David's story has been told. But God's story is not complete. The main character must intrude upon the action one more time, if for no other reason than to reassert divine presence in the story and in the world.

Second Samuel 24 is a candid portrait of the God that has moved in and out of the Deuteronomic History. It presents to us a God that still feels. God is angry in v. 1. We are not sure why, but we know the anger is real. This anthropomorphic aspect of God's nature has always kept the divine unpredictable. At

> **Who Inspired the Census?**
> Compare the very different versions of the Deuteronomist and the Chronicler:
>
> | *2 Samuel 24:1* | *1 Chronicles 21:1* |
> |---|---|
> | Again the anger of the LORD was kindled against Israel, and he incited David against them, saying, "Go, count the people of Israel and Judah." | Satan stood up against Israel, and incited David to count the people of Israel. |
>
> To these opposing explanations, we should also add the words of 2 Sam 24:10, in which David himself assumes full responsibility for making the decision to conduct a census: "But afterward, David was stricken to the heart because he had numbered the people. David said to the LORD, 'I have sinned greatly in what I have done. But now, O LORD, I pray you, take away the guilt of your servant; for I have done very foolishly'" (compare also 24:17).
>
> What is clear is that David took a census. It is likely that he decided to do this on his own because it was good governmental policy. To Israel's theological historians, however, it was poor sacerdotal policy, a violation of trust in Yahweh. The Deuteronomistic editors begin the story with Yahweh's anger at some unnamed sin (or collection of sins) in Israel. Such sin cried out for punishment, but for the judgment to be understood as coming from Yahweh, a more focused catalytic event was needed. Thus, the Deuteronomist credited Yahweh with inciting David to order the census for the express purpose of provoking punishment (cf. Yahweh's hardening Pharaoh's heart in Exod 7–9 or the divine disinformation given the prophets of Ahab in 1 Kgs 22:19-23).
>
> The Chronicler was no longer comfortable with the idea that God might incite someone to sin in order to set them up as a public illustration of the Deuteronomistic claim that wickedness must be punished. So the Chronicler insists that it was not Yahweh, but Satan, who inspired David to take a census (1 Chr 21:1). The word *śātān* is the same as in the book of Job, except that in 1 Chr 21:1 it has no definite article, as it characteristically does in Job 1:6-12; 2:1-6. Thus, while Job uses *haśśātān* as a title for a heavenly district attorney ("The Accuser"), in Chronicles "Satan" seems to have become a proper name for one who leads humankind into evil. This concept continued to develop in the postexilic period and was popularly accepted in the New Testament.
>
> Thus, the theological and historical perspectives of the tradents have influenced their opinion of whether Yahweh or Satan incited David to number Israel. The most likely scenario is that David made the decision on his own, while later interpreters debated whether he did so under divine or demonic inspiration.

times, God's feelings work to Israel's favor. Prior to the exodus experience, God heard the cries of his people, saw their misery, and knew their suffering (Exod 3:7-8). These divine observations produced compassion in the heart of God.

On the other hand, in 2 Samuel 6, David celebratively returns the ark of the covenant to Jerusalem. Uzzah, who walked beside the ark as it was pulled on an ox cart, reached up to steady the ark when the cart hit a bump. God's anger was immediately kindled against him and God struck him dead. We wish we knew everything that made God angry. We wish we could predict when grace would give way to anger. We wish we knew why God was angry in 2 Samuel 24. If we knew these things, then God would be a bit more predictable . . . and within our control. But these things are not ours to know. God feels. And God's feelings are not to be manipulated.

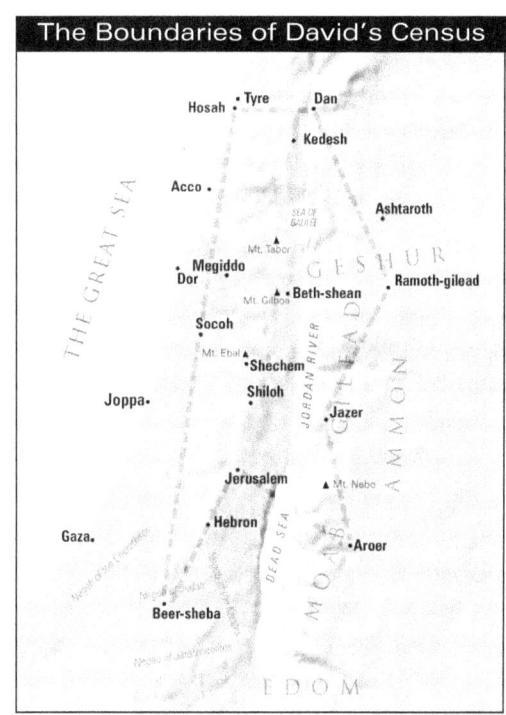

Second Samuel 24 affirms that God is still active. Verse 1 continues by stating that "(God) incited David . . ." God incites David to perform an act that God considers sinful. God is still active in this narrative drama, but in a way that makes us uncomfortable. This thought is so uncomfortable that a later historian retells the story in 1 Chronicles 21 and credits Satan with David's prompting.

This apparently problematic text is not outside the boundaries of Hebrew thought, however. It was God that hardened the heart of Pharaoh—an act that would later lead to Pharaoh's punishment. And later, in 1 Kings 22, God sends a lying spirit to entice Ahab into a war that leads to Ahab's demise. Second Samuel ends with the strong assertion that the God of Israel does not operate within our boundaries; God is free, unpredictable, beyond understanding, and dangerous.[3]

This text also reminds us that God still defends. Verses 2-9 reveal the content of God's incitement. God has prompted David to take a census of Israel. Although Joab, David's confidant and primary military strategist, questions the act, David persists and proceeds.

It is commonly acknowledged that the primary purpose of taking a census in the ancient world was for the collection of taxes and the conscription of an army.[4] It appears God was testing David's confidence in God's ability to defend. Taxation and the expansion of the military would undergird the institutional structure established under David's rule. But what role would God have in this

Pestilence, Sword, and Famine

The death-dealing trio of pestilence, sword, and famine frequently appears together in Scripture, especially in the prophecies of Jeremiah and Ezekiel. Both prophets commonly predicted that Yahweh would send punishment upon Israel in the form of pestilence, sword, and famine. For example, Jeremiah threatened the population of Judah who remained under Zedekiah, saying "And I will send sword, famine, and pestilence upon them, until they are utterly destroyed from the land that I gave to them and their ancestors" (Jer 24:10; see also Jer 14:12; 15:2; 18:21; 21:7, 9; 27:8, 13; 29:17-18; 32:24, 36; 34:17; 38:2; 42:17, 22; 44:13).

Ezekiel declared against Jerusalem that "One third of you shall die of pestilence or be consumed by famine among you; one third shall fall by the sword around you; and one third I will scatter to every wind and will unsheathe the sword after them" (Ezek 5:12; see also Ezek 5:17; 6:11-12; 7:15; 12:16; 14:21).

In the light of these dire predictions, it seems a mercy that David was given the chance to choose only one member of the lethal trio.

new structure? Are we approaching the prophetic point of which Samuel warned (1 Sam 8:10-17)? When calling for a monarchy, the Israelites dreamed of a king who would fight their battles. They imagined an institution that would insure their defense. Was God's incitement of David indeed a test to determine David's level of belief in God's ability to defend?

God is not pleased with David's choice, and therefore, punishment ensues. In vv. 10-14, God offers David three options for punishment through Gad, the prophet. David may choose three years of famine, three months of enemy pursuit, or three days of pestilence at the hand of God. As Samuel had prophesied (1 Sam 12:13-15), the actions of the king would be suffered or enjoyed by the people at large. Each of the options for punishment placed the people at great risk.

David's choice? He chooses three days of pestilence. Why? "[L]et us fall into the hands of the LORD, for his mercy is great; but let us not fall into human hands." During a three-year famine, the people of Israel would be at the mercy of their neighbors' generosity. During three months of enemy pursuit, they would be at the mercy of their adversary's sword. David chooses to fall into the unpredictable and dangerous hand of God. For David knows that while God cannot be controlled, God is committed to Israel. Neighbors and enemies are predictably stingy and hostile. But with God, there is hope for mercy.

The final affirmation of this text is that God is the best source of mercy. David's choice proves to be a wise one. In vv. 15-25, the record of David's punishment and Israel's punishment is preserved. An angel of the Lord moves from Dan to Beersheba killing seventy thousand Israelites. And just as the angel is about to pour its pestilence upon Jerusalem, God mercifully intervenes.

The Destroyer

Yahweh's agent of destruction is described in v. 16 as "the angel" (*hammalʾāk*), as "the angel who was bringing destruction among the people" (*hammalʾāk hammašḥît bāʿām*) and as "the angel of Yahweh" (*malʾāk YHWH*). *Malʾāk* is the Hebrew word for "messenger" or "envoy." The Greek translation is *angelos*, leading to the modern translation as "angel." The envoy of Yahweh was a heavenly being sent to do the work of Yahweh—in this case a destructive work. A similar agent of divine destruction appears in the story of the death of the firstborn in Exod 12:23. There the heavenly envoy is called "the destroyer" (*hammašḥît*).

Some recent interpreters relate the account to an ancient story associated with a non-Israelite god such as Resheph, the Canaanite god of pestilence. The Mesopotamians also had such a god (Nergal), and the Greeks assigned destructive functions to Apollo. The name Resheph may be derived from the word for "fire," presumably because of the fevers associated with many illnesses associated with plague. Numerous written sources from ancient Mesopotamia (3rd millennium BC) and later from the Ugaritic city of Ras-Shamra testify to the popularity of the cult of Resheph. There is evidence that the cult also existed in Egypt during the eighteenth dynasty (1546–1310 BC). Israel was thus surrounded by and intermingled with populations who worshiped Resheph. In 1 Chr 7:25, an Israelite is named Resheph, and in Deut 32:24 and Ps 78:48, the word *rešep* is used with the meaning "pestilence."

These factors suggest a familiarity with the cult of Resheph in Israel, but the association of the avenging angel with Yahweh is too strong to presume that a Resheph tradition underlies the present story, where Yahweh is emphatically in control from beginning to end.

This unpredictable God *repents*. No more explanation is given for God's mercy than was previously given for God's anger.[5]

David responds to this act of mercy with a second prayer of confession and repentance. At the insistence of Gad, David purchases the threshing floor of Araunah, builds an altar there, and offers burnt offerings and peace offerings to God. After the presentation of these offerings, the narrator concludes the story and book in v. 25 by saying, "So the LORD answered [David's] supplication for the land, and the plague was averted from Israel." David's sacrifice was in no way manipulative because mercy had already been dispensed. These final words do imply, however, that David's prayers and eventual obedience were essential elements for God's continued mercy.

The Books of Samuel conclude with God asserting himself as the main character of this historic narrative. Although there are moments when God seems absent from Israel's text and timeline, God still feels, acts, and provides the best source of defense and mercy for Israel. God will not be controlled, but Israel can be assured that God is committed. That assurance would speak volumes to an Israelite held captive in Babylon.

Second Samuel 24 is hardly an unnecessary appendix to this portion of Israel's history. It was necessary to reiterate these aspects of God's nature that had slowly slipped from Israel's stories. The God who felt the pain and fear of Israel in Egypt seems emotionally uninvolved in much of 2 Samuel. The God who actively parted the Red Sea and empowered Samson seems silent and still as the Davidic narrative progresses. In 2 Samuel 21, David is assisted by his mighty men in killing the giant, Ishbibenob. Where is the God of slingshot and stone who defended Israel in days past? Prior to 2 Samuel 24, God has slowly been written out of the drama.

The spiritual tension created by God's waning presence and haunting absence is clear to the careful reader of the broader text. God's diminishing role in the life of Israel can be vividly seen in symbol, word, and action.

The primary symbol of God's presence throughout the Books of Samuel is the ark of the covenant. This sacred box was constructed at Mt. Sinai following the Israelites' exodus from Egypt. Made of acacia wood, with a removable top adorned with two golden cherubim, the ark contained the stone tablets of the Ten Commandments. There is little doubt the Israelites equated this ark with the very presence of God. The "Song of the Ark" in Numbers 10:35-36 suggests that Moses addressed the ark as an embodiment of the Lord.

The ark seems to have a literary life of its own. Scholars refer to stories about the ark in 1 and 2 Samuel as "The Ark Narratives." These stories, which often appear independent of the narrative flow of the books, were probably woven into the Deuteronomic History from another source.[6] In these stories, the ark serves as the "main character," with humanity taking a lesser role. Equating the ark with the presence of God provides us one method of tracing the diminishing role of God within Israel's written history.

The Ark of the Covenant

The ark was a portable sanctuary from Israel's wilderness days (see Exod 25:10-15). The ark was the place of God's special presence among the people, guiding them through the wilderness. It also served to house the two tablets of the Law (Deut 10:8) and hence had a specific link to the Sinai covenant. David recaptured the ark from the Philistines, brought it to Jerusalem, and built a house for it (2 Sam 4–6). This was a means that David used to unify the northern and southern tribes. King Solomon brought it into the Holy of Holies of the temple, where it symbolized not only the place of God, but the throne of God in the midst of his people (1 Kgs 8:1-13). The ark was probably destroyed by the Babylonians when they razed the temple, but no specific mention is made of its destruction.

The ark reportedly was carried before the people when they crossed the Jordan River into the land of Canaan. It was instrumental in the conquering of Jericho and other besieged cities in the promised land (Josh 6–7). At the end of this period of conquest and rule by the judges, the ark was placed in the care of Eli in Shiloh.[7] These early stories affirmed God's presence and power in relation to the ark.

In the Books of Samuel, we observe strange twists in the life of the ark. In 1 Samuel 4, the Israelites are defeated in a battle against the Philistines. They surmised that their defeat was caused by the absence of the ark. They retrieve the ark in v. 5, attack the Philistines again in v. 10, and this time the Philistines beat the Israelites *and* capture the ark! Eli was so astonished at this twist of fate that upon hearing of the ark's capture, he fell out of his chair, broke his neck, and died (1 Sam 4:18). This incident in the ark narrative provides an early hint that God is free and cannot be controlled.

While the Philistines have ownership of the ark, each city to which it is carried suffers a plague (1 Sam 6). Eventually, they decide to surrender the ark to the Israelites, carrying it to the house of Abinadab. From 1 Samuel 6 to 2 Samuel 6, there are no references to the ark. But in the eighth year of David's reign, he brought the ark to Jerusalem, his capital city. His first attempt to transport the ark ended in the death of Uzzah, a seemingly innocent bystander. Drawn on an ox cart, the ark began to rock when the cart hit a bump. Uzzah reached up to steady the ark and God struck him dead (a fairly vivid reminder that God will not be controlled). David placed the ark at the home of Obededom for three months. Then with pomp and parade, he had the ark safely and appropriately carried into Jerusalem—not by oxen, but by men.

When in Jerusalem, the ark was placed in a tent (2 Sam 7:2). It did accompany David into a war against the Ammonites (2 Sam 11:1), but David eventually ordered it taken back to Jerusalem. There is no further record of its presence in the battles of Israel. Later, in 1 Kings 8, Solomon places the ark in the inner chamber of the temple—the holy of holies. There is no further mention of the ark in the Deuteronomic History. This furnishing, which once embodied the powerful presence of God, apparently became an enshrined religious relic, and at some point it was lost. Symbolically, God's role diminished.

We also see the gradual decrease of God's presence in the reduced frequency of God's speech. The presence and absence of "God's word" speaks as loudly as the presence and absence of God's symbol. The short phrase "And the Lord said" comprises four percent of Hebrew vocabulary.[8] Within the exodus narratives, the phrase appears eighty-one times: fifty-three times in the Book of Exodus and twenty-eight times in the Book of Numbers.

In the books attributed to the Deuteronomic Historian, however, the speech of the Lord God becomes less frequent. The phrase appears fifteen times in the Book of Deuteronomy, fifteen times in Joshua, fourteen times in Judges, thirteen times in 1 Samuel, and only four times in 2 Samuel. Of the seventeen total occurrences of this phrase in 1 and 2 Samuel, eight of them are in dialogue to Samuel in the early chapters of 1 Samuel. The phrase appears only once in the last four chapters of 2 Samuel. While the frequency of the phrase is not a scientific method of defining the limits of God's actual verbal exchanges in Israel's history, it at least suggests the writer's awareness that divine communication was in decline.

In addition to the symbol and word, God's visibly recorded activity declined in the life of Israel. Prior to 1 Samuel 12, God is immanently intrusive in the drama of His world. It is not uncommon for God to intrude upon the affairs of humans. God creates humanity, punishes humanity, floods the world, cuts covenants with Abraham's family, delivers a nation, parts a sea, provides a land, empowers judges, blesses a barren woman, and even appoints kings. But after the reign of Saul gets underway in 1 Samuel 13, there is much less divine activity. In the words of Old Testament scholar David Jobling, "Saul seems to inhabit a less God-filled world."[9]

This spiraling diminishment of the presence of God in symbol, word, and action comes to an abrupt halt in 2 Samuel 24. At the end of the Davidic narrative, God bursts back on the scene, full of feeling, ready for action, able to defend, and willing to be merciful. God unpredictably and mysteriously intrudes upon the life of David and displays a willingness to be committed but not controlled.

TENSIONS IN LIFE

While 2 Samuel 24 may seem an unnecessary appendage to some, it no doubt held remarkable hope for the exiled Israelite. The captive Jewish population had already interpreted their exile as punishment. They had already come to grips with the apparent absence of God. God's feelings, actions, defense, and mercy seemed miles away in memories of their homeland. But in 2 Samuel 24, the

Israelites are reminded that even in God's anger, there is the possibility—even the probability—of merciful presence.

This presence cannot be controlled, however. God could not be manipulated through the possession of the ark; both Israel and the Philistines suffered during ownership. God could not be controlled through even the most heartfelt prayers of the faithful; Samuel's complaint of monarchy only led to God's appointment of the first king. God would not succumb to the utilitarian motivations of Israel's worship. As Samuel said to Saul, "Has the LORD as great delight in burnt offerings and sacrifices, as in obedience to the voice of the LORD? Surely, to obey is better than sacrifice" (1 Sam 15:22).

Maybe after years of exile and hearing these stories over and over again, Israel finally learned the premiere lesson of human existence—we are servants of God, not vice versa. We exist for God's whims and not God for ours. We are at God's beck and call; God is not at ours. God is God. The God of Israel is committed to us but will not be controlled.

Each of the tensions we've encountered in 1 and 2 Samuel compose a part of the mystery of God. God's embrace and rejection of political systems, the fine line God carves between works and grace, the push God gives the underdog, and the fluctuating sense of God's presence and absence—all speak to the mysterious tensions inherent in human relationship with the divine. These tensions keep God beyond our understanding. They keep us from reducing God to a manageable and predictable deity. They prevent us from carving an idol in our mind that resembles the God we wish God to be. The political, theological, relational, and spiritual tensions of these texts ensure that God was and is and will always be a sovereign mystery.

CONVEYING THE TENSION

Guiding the Worshiper

Synopsis of Worship Theme
It would not be an overstatement to say that every believer has experienced a sense of both the absence and presence of God. We tend, however, to celebrate God's presence corporately and suffer God's absence alone.

This particular worship service provides opportunity for affirming God's presence and sharing the sense of God's absence. While the service seems short in comparison to other suggested services in this book, it is purposefully structured to allow for an element of spontaneity that is often time-consuming. It appears less liturgical in nature. But since liturgy refers to "the work of the people," you will find this service just as liturgical since the people have to work just as hard.

Within the section titled "God With Us in the Past," worshipers are encouraged to share testimonies of God's presence in their life in days past. Prior to the service, you may wish to ask one or two members to begin the time of sharing. Allow a moderate amount of time for others to share. Within the section titled "God With Us in the Present," worshipers are encouraged to speak their prayer requests and participate in a time of silent prayer prior to the Pastoral Prayer. Highlighting and vocalizing the needs of people will remind the church of moments when God seems absent in our lives. You may wish to encourage your members simply to speak the name of the person they wish to be remembered in prayer. This will help manage time restraints to which you must adhere. If there are no time restraints, parishioners may share more freely.

Insure throughout each movement of the service that the focus is on the role of God within the life of the believer and the church. Take every opportunity to affirm God's commitment to his people and his uncontrollable sovereignty in the world.

Suggested Order of Worship

GOD WITH US IN THE PAST
Organ Prelude
Chiming of the Hour
The Epistle Lesson   Hebrews 1:1-4
Hymn of Praise 355   "For All the Saints"   SINE NOMINE
Invocation
Welcome of Worshipers
Hymn of Testimony 531   "Redeemed"   ADA
Testimonies of God's Presence

GOD WITH US IN THE PRESENT
The Gospel Lesson   Matthew 7:7-11
Hymn of Petition 20   "Sing Praise to God Who Reigns Above"   MIT FREUDEN ZART

The Needs of the People

The Prayers of the People
The Pastoral Prayer
Hymn of Offering 19   "We Praise You, O God, Our Redeemer"   KREMSER
Offertory Prayer
Offertory
The Doxology

GOD WITH US IN THE FUTURE

The Old Testament Lesson   2 Samuel 24
Choral Anthem
Message
Hymn of Decision 54   "Great is Thy Faithfulness"   FAITHFULNESS
Benediction
Choral Response
Organ Postlude

Musical Options

Instrumental Music:
  A Mighty Fortress, Ovid Young (piano)
  Great Is Thy Faithfulness, Melody Bober (piano)
  How Firm a Foundation, Don Hustad (organ)

Choral Music:
  God of Grace and God of Glory, Langston, SATB, Brodt Music, No 513
  The Majesty and Glory of Your Name, Fettke, SATB, Word Music, CS-2954
  How Great Thou Art, arr. Courtney, SATB, Beckenhorst Press, BP 1440

Sermon Outlines

Meeting God Again: 2 Samuel 24 (An Expository Outline)

After ten years in the real world, my high school graduating class celebrated its reunion. Many of us had sporadically kept in touch, but few of us had spent the kind of time together we had during our academic days. It was a joy to see one another. We had obviously changed externally. But we had changed internally, as well. It was interesting to converse about values, feelings, and the variety of life experiences that had shaped us through the decade. There were also things we had forgotten about one another and the ten-year "refresher course" was an informative delight.

There are periods of time when we seem distanced from God. It is always good to refresh our relationship with Him. We will remember things we have forgotten and learn things we never knew. This was true in the life of David and true years later in the life of exiled Israel. Today's text reacquainted them with:

I. A God that Feels (v. 1a)
II. A God that Acts (vv. 1b-9)
III. A God that Converses (vv. 10-14)
IV. A God that Extends Mercy (vv. 15-16)
V. A God that Deserves Worship (vv. 17-25)

The Main Character: 2 Samuel 24 (A Narrative Sermon)
(The speaker should use information gleaned from earlier chapters in this study to formulate the narrative movements of this sermon. There is room for flexibility and direction.)

Who is the main character of 1 and 2 Samuel? In this period during Israel's history, who is the dominant actor?

I. Samuel? The book is named for him and he ushers Israel through a time of political tension.
II. Saul? He is the first king of Israel and he endures the chastisement of change.
III. David? He is a king after God's own heart who establishes Israel as a viable and powerful force in the world.
IV. God? God is the one who is always present, helping us to survive all the tensions of our lives.

Guiding the Learner

The Occurrence
We have discussed at length the diminishing role of God in the Books of 1 and 2 Samuel. You may wish to use the following outline to introduce your students to this "late intrusion" of God into the text. The outline highlights those mysterious attributes of God with which David (and eventually the exilic reader) became reacquainted.

I. God's mysterious emotions (v. 1a)
II. God's mysterious activity (vv. 1b-9)
III. God's mysterious voice (vv. 10-14)
IV. God's mysterious grace (vv. 15-16)
V. God's mysterious presence (vv. 17-25)

One could also outline David's role in responding to a mysterious God. This alternative outline demonstrates how intricately our lives are woven within the fabric of God's actions. It would be helpful to note that David does not control or even fully understand God's actions. David simply does what any human is able to do.

I. David is tempted by a mysterious God. (v. 1)
II. David makes a choice. (vv. 2-9)
III. David confesses. (v. 10)
IV. David makes a choice. (vv. 11-16)
V. David confesses. (v. 17)
VI. David worships a mysterious God. (vv. 18-25)

The Memory
C. S. Lewis was a great author and a lover of great books. In his letters to Arthur Greeves he once wrote, "I can't imagine a man really enjoying a book and reading it only once."[10] It is not uncommon for me to finish a book and then spend days rereading and reflecting upon significant lines and paragraphs.

Imagine that you are an exiled Israelite in Babylon. You have just finished reading 1 and 2 Samuel. As you reflect upon this collection of stories, think about the following questions.

• What stories have you read that helped you understand the feelings of God?
• In what ways did people try to control God?
• In what ways did God exercise freedom?
• How do these stories about God offer hope to an exile?

The Interpretation
Symbols

Like the Israelites with the ark of the covenant, Christianity has symbols of faith that convey the presence and power of God. These symbols are embraced in differing degrees by different denominations. Some people view these symbols as relics of days gone by and others view them as powerful mediums of God's presence.

- How do Protestants and Catholics differ in their views of the Lord's Supper?
- Is there a limit to the presence and power conveyed by communion?
- How do different communities of faith interpret baptism?
- How and to what extent is God's presence and power conveyed in each faith system?

Journaling

Many people keep a journal or diary of their faith experiences.

- How does (or would) your journal convey your perceived "closeness" to God?
- Are there times when feel that God is absent?
- What questions and affirmations do those moments raise in your mind?
- When have you most strongly felt God's presence and absence?

Control

The Israelites attempted to control God's presence and power through their use of the ark of the covenant, ritualistic sacrifices, and an over-reliance upon the grace of the Davidic covenant.

- How do people try to control or manipulate God today?
- Is it possible to use prayer or worship as an instrument of manipulation?
- How do we take advantage of God's grace in our living and decision-making?

NOTES

[1] Eugene H. Peterson, *First and Second Samuel* (Louisville: Westminster, John Knox Press, 1999), 91.

[2] R. P Gordon, *1 & 2 Samuel* (Sheffield England: Sheffield Academic Press Ltd., 1998), 95.

[3] Walter Brueggemann, *First and Second Samuel,* Interpretation, A Bible Commentary for Preaching and Teaching (Louisville: John Knox Press, 1990), 351.

[4] P. Kyle McCarter Jr., *II Samuel*, The Anchor Bible (New York: Doubleday, 1984), 514.

[5] Brueggemann, 353.

[6] Tony W. Cartledge, *I & II Samuel*, Smyth and Helwys Bible Commentary (Macon: Smyth and Helwys Publishing, Inc., 2001), 69.

[7] G. Henton Davies, "Ark of the Covenant," *The Interpreter's Dictionary of the Bible* (Nashville: Abingdon Press, 1984), 223.

[8] Bonnie Pedrotti Kittel, Vicki Hoffer, and Rebecca Abts Wright, *Biblical Hebrew, A Text and Workbook* (New Haven and London: Yale University Press, 1989), 8.

[9] David Jobling, *I Samuel*, Berit Olam, Studies in Hebrew Narrative and Poetry (Collegeville: The Liturgical Press, 1988), 257.

[10] Walter Hooper, ed. *The Letters of C. S. Lewis to Arthur Greeves (1914-1963)* (New York: Collier/Mcmillan, 1986), 439.

TEACHING 1 & 2 SAMUEL TO CHILDREN

WHEN I AM AFRAID

The Books of 1 and 2 Samuel are among those written and shared by the Israelites while in Babylonian exile. The stories in these books became a source of hope and comfort for people separated from their homeland.

One can only imagine the fears and anxieties the Israelite children must have felt during this era in their history. This series of lessons presents 1 and 2 Samuel as a collection of stories that may have addressed the fears of children. As is consistent with Hebrew tradition, these stories would allow parents to communicate God's past faithfulness to their children, as well as assure their children of God's faithfulness for the future.

Outline of Sessions and Texts
Session 1: When I Am Afraid, God Answers Prayer
1 Samuel 1

Session 2: When I Am Afraid, I Remember God Is Strong
1 Samuel 17:17-51

Session 3: When I Am Afraid, I Depend on My Friends
1 Samuel 20

Session 4: When I Am Afraid, I Remember God's Promises
2 Samuel 7:1-17

Session 5: When I Am Afraid, I Worship God
2 Samuel 22

Session 1

WHEN I AM AFRAID, GOD ANSWERS PRAYER

1 SAMUEL 1

Teacher's Introduction

As we consider the stories of 1 and 2 Samuel, we imagine that these stories of life and faith may have been shared between the Israelite parents and their children as a way to calm fears and encourage faith. In this first session on "When I Am Afraid," we look at God's faithfulness shown to us through answered prayer.

In this lesson, your children will examine their fears and share ways that they find peace and comfort. They will also explore the importance of prayer as a way of communicating with God and as a way of sharing their fears and concerns with God. They will learn that God is faithful to listen and respond to their prayers in accordance with his will and plan for their lives.

Introductory Activity: Who's Calling?

Materials: *Plastic cups, string cut into lengths approximately five feet long, slips of paper with the words "God answers prayer" written on each one (one slip per child)*

Before the Session: Make a small center hole in the bottom of each cup. Then push the string through the holes of two cups, and tie the ends into knots so the cups are connected. When the string is pulled taut, it can carry sound waves from one cup to another. Make one set of cups for every two children in your group.

Place the children in pairs. Give each pair one set of the cup phones, and demonstrate how they work. One child should hold a cup to his/her ear while another child speaks into the second cup. Allow the children time to practice talking into their phones, then distribute the prepared slips of paper to each child. Ask them not to reveal what is on their paper, but tell them that it is a special message for them to share with their friend. Using the phones, have each child speak the special message ("God answers prayer") to his/her partner. When the children complete the activity, talk with them about today's session: "When I Am Afraid, God Answers Prayer." Ask them how we can talk to God. Do we need telephones or other special devices? Ponder with them how we know God hears us when we pray. Assure the children that God hears us because we trust him, and he has promised always to be with us. God knows all of our thoughts and feelings, our wants and needs. Ask the children about their own prayers. Do they talk to God? Do they have a special time or place to talk to God? How do they talk to God? Tell the children that today we will learn about a woman named Hannah who talked to God.

Introduction of 1 & 2 Samuel

You may wish to give your children an overview of 1 and 2 Samuel and how they will be studied in these sessions.

1. Ask the children to find the books of 1 and 2 Samuel in their Bibles, assisting as needed. Emphasize that these books are found in the Old Testament.

2. Tell your class that 1 and 2 Samuel were written and shared by the Israelite people while they were in Babylonian exile. Talk with the children about what it means to be in exile. The Israelites lived far from their homeland and were treated as slaves in Babylon, and the stories in 1 and 2 Samuel helped bring comfort and hope to them. Israelite moms and dads may have used these stories to help their children when they were afraid. The stories remind children that God is always with them and always watching over them. Encourage discussion by asking questions similar to the following:

- Have you ever been away from home?
- Have you ever been afraid when you were away from home?
- How did you feel?

- What kind of place makes you afraid?
- What do you do to make yourself feel better when you are afraid?

3. Introduce the story for Session 1. Remind the children that the Israelites were in a strange land. They remembered God's faithfulness by sharing stories, and they probably prayed to God when they were afraid. Chapter 1 of 1 Samuel tells the story of Hannah, a woman who prayed to God. God answered Hannah's prayer, just as God answers our prayers.

Biblical Lesson: 1 Samuel 1

Materials: *Copies of the biblical lesson for the children who will read the parts of Elkanah, Hannah, and Eli*

Before the Session: The Bible lesson is written as a narrative for you to do with your children. You may choose a child to read the part of the narrator, or you may plan to do this part yourself. Choose children to read the parts of Elkanah, Hannah, and Eli. Make copies of the narrative for the children who will read aloud. Another option is to use a Bible storybook or tell the story in your own words.

1 Samuel 1:10—Hannah's prayer was a bitter but hopeful cry for help.

Julius Schnoor von Carolsfeld. *Hannah's Prayer.* 19th century. Woodcut. *Das Buch der Bucher in Bilden.* (Credit: Dover Pictorial Archive Series)

Hannah's Prayer

Narrator: There was a certain man from the hill country of Ephraim, whose name was Elkanah. He had two wives; one was called Hannah and the other Peninnah. Peninnah had children, but Hannah had none.

Year after year this man went up from his town to worship and sacrifice to the LORD at Shiloh. Whenever the day came for Elkanah to sacrifice, he would give portions of the meat to his wife Peninnah and to all her sons and daughters. But to Hannah he gave two portions because he loved her and because she had no children. And because she had no children, Peninnah kept irritating her. This went on year after year. Whenever Hannah went up to the house of the LORD, Peninnah bothered her until she cried and would not eat. Elkanah, her husband, would say to her,

Elkanah: "Hannah, why are you crying? Why don't you eat? Why are you sad? Don't I mean more to you than ten sons?"

Narrator: Once when they had finished eating and drinking in Shiloh, Hannah stood up. Now Eli the priest was sitting on a chair by the door of the LORD's temple. With bitterness in her heart Hannah cried a lot and prayed to the LORD. And she made a vow, saying,

Hannah: "O LORD Almighty, if you will only look upon your servant's misery and remember me, and not forget your servant but give her a son, then I will give him to the LORD for all the days of his life."

Narrator: As she kept on praying to the LORD, Eli observed her mouth. Hannah was praying in her heart, and her lips were moving but her voice was not heard. Eli thought she was drunk and said to her,

Eli: "How long will you keep on getting drunk? Get rid of your wine."

Hannah: "Not so, my lord. I am a woman who is deeply troubled. I have not been drinking wine or beer; I was pouring out my soul to the LORD. Do not take your servant for a wicked woman; I have been praying here out of my great anguish and grief."

Eli: "Go in peace, and may the God of Israel grant you what you have asked of him."

Hannah: "May your servant find favor in your eyes."

Narrator: Then she went her way and ate something, and her face was no longer downcast.
　Early the next morning they arose and worshiped before the LORD and then went back to their home. So in the course of time Hannah and Elkanah had a son. She named him Samuel, saying,

Hannah: "Because I asked the LORD for him."

Review Questions: Ask the following or similar questions to your class for review and to guide them in their understanding of this story. After each question, allow for responses and discussion.

- Why was Hannah sad?
- What did she do when she was sad and upset?
- How did Hannah pray?
- Did she need a phone or some other special device to talk to God?
- Did God answer Hannah's prayer?
- How did God answer Hannah's prayer?

How Does God Answer Your Prayers?

Materials: *Posterboard, markers*

Before the Session: Place the children into small groups of three or four per group. Write, or ask them to write, the heading "Prayers Asked" on the left side of the posterboard. Draw a line down the center and on the right side write the heading "Prayers Answered."

Have the children think of prayers that they or their families have asked God to answer, and record them under the heading "Prayers Asked." In the other column, write how God answered their prayer. Remind the children that sometimes the way God answers prayer may not be the way that we want him to answer our prayers. After each group has had a chance to finish their posters, allow them to share their answers with the entire group.

Memory Verse Activity: Prayer Journals

"The LORD has heard my cry for mercy; the LORD accepts my prayer." (Psalm 6:8)

Materials: *Construction paper, white copying paper, markers, pencils, stapler*

Before the Session: Make small booklets for each child. Fold a sheet of construction paper in half, then fold two sheets of white copying paper inside the construction paper and staple together. Print the memory verse on a marker board or poster and display it in your room.

Give each child a prepared booklet. Tell the class that they will make prayer journals to take home and use. Ask them to write the memory verse on the cover, then decorate their prayer journal with the markers. Encourage the children to take their prayer journals home and write down their prayers and the way God answers them.

Pray

Assure the children that when they are afraid or unsure, God will always hear them when they call on him.

Say a prayer together, asking God to help us know that he hears our prayers.

Thank God for hearing us when we pray and for answering our prayers in the way that is best for us.

Session 2

WHEN I AM AFRAID, I REMEMBER GOD IS STRONG

1 SAMUEL 17:17-51

Teacher's Introduction

In 1 Samuel 17:17-51 we find the story of the young David and the Philistine champion, Goliath. In this familiar story your children witness a young boy who used the might and power that God gave him to defeat a giant. This lesson guides children to understand that God is stronger than anything, and that his strength can be used in their lives to defeat their fears and foes when they trust in him.

Introductory Activity: "These Things Are Strong" Collage

Materials: *Old magazines that can be cut, scissors for each child, glue, posterboard, a strip of posterboard or construction paper*

Before the Session: Write the heading "These Things Are Strong" at the top of the piece posterboard. On the strip of posterboard write the phrase "But God Is Stronger!"

Lay out the magazines, scissors, glue, and prepared poster in a place accessible to the children. Ask the children to look through the magazines for pictures of things that they think are strong or pictures of things that make people strong. Have them cut the pictures from the magazines and glue them onto the posterboard to make a collage.

When the children complete their collage, ask them to tell you about the pictures they have chosen. Talk with them about why they chose certain pictures, affirming their choices of things that are strong. Then remind the children that

God is stronger than any of these things! Tape the strip of paper with the words "But God Is Stronger!" across the collage.

Introduction of 1 Samuel 17:17-51

Talk with the children about today's session: "When I Am Afraid, I Remember God Is Strong." Tell them that they will hear a story about a young boy named David. David allowed God's strength to work in him to do something great.

Biblical Lesson: 1 Samuel 17:17-51

Before the Session: This lesson is written as a monologue for David. For this lesson you could choose someone from your class to present it, or ask a youth or young adult to come and present the monologue in biblical costume. Another option is to use a Bible storybook or tell the story in your own words.

David's Monologue:
Hello, my name is David. I am the son of Jesse, an Ephrathite from Bethlehem in Judah. My father had eight sons, and I am the youngest. My three oldest brothers went to war with King Saul to fight the Philistines. While they were off fighting, I was left to tend my father's sheep in Bethlehem.

Sometimes I was allowed to run errands for my father. These errands took me to the camp where my brothers were fighting. One of my errands to the camp found me in an interesting situation. Let me tell you about a very big day in my life.

My father called to me on that day and said, "David, take this roasted grain and these ten loaves of bread for your brothers and hurry to their camp. Take along these ten cheeses to the commander of their unit. See how your brothers are doing and report back to me that I may know they are safe. They are with Saul and all the men of Israel in the Valley of Elah, fighting against the Philistines."

So early in the morning I left the flock with a shepherd, loaded up, and set out as my father had told me. I reached the camp as the army was going out to battle. Israel and the Philistines were ready to face each other in battle. I left my things with the keeper of supplies, ran to the battle lines, and greeted my brothers.

As I was talking to my brothers, the Philistine champion named Goliath stepped out and shouted out his battle cry. Goliath was no ordinary soldier.

He was the biggest and strongest soldier I had ever seen. He stood over nine feet tall and wore battle armor from his head to his toes. When the Israelites saw him, they all ran away in fear.

Now the Israelites were all saying, "Do you see this man, how he keeps coming out? He comes out to defy Israel. The king will give great wealth to the man who kills him. He will also give him his daughter in marriage and his father's family can stop paying taxes in Israel." I thought that sounded quite interesting, so I asked the men standing near me what would happen for the one who defeated Goliath.

When my oldest brother heard me talking to the men, he became very angry with me and asked me, "Why have you come down here?" I didn't mean to anger my brother, but I believed that I could defeat the great Goliath.

The men who had heard me talking took me before Saul and I said to him, "Let no one be scared because of Goliath: I will go and fight him." Saul said to me, "You are not able to go out against this giant and fight him; you are only a boy, and he is a great and accomplished soldier." I said to Saul, "I have killed both lions and bears while tending my father's flocks; Goliath will be like one of them, because he has defied the armies of the living God. The LORD who delivered me from the paw of the lion and the bear will deliver me from Goliath."

Saul said to me, "Go, and the LORD be with you." Well, God was with me. Saul and his men dressed me for battle, but I said to them, "I cannot wear these, because I am not used to them." So I took the staff in my hand, chose five smooth stones, put them in the pouch of my shepherd's bag, and with my sling I approached Goliath.

Goliath saw that I was only a boy and made fun of me. He said bad things about my God, but I said to him, "You come against me with sword and spear, but I come against you in the name of the LORD Almighty, the God of the armies of Israel."

Then I ran quickly to the battle line. I reached into my bag and took out a stone, slung it, and struck old Goliath on the forehead. The stone sank into his forehead, and he fell facedown on the ground.

I knew that Goliath was a strong man, but I knew that God was even stronger. I trusted God to make me strong, and I was able to defeat that giant. When you face fears and enemies, you must also trust God to be strong for you.

Review Questions: Ask the following or similar questions to your class for review and to guide them in their understanding of the story. After each question, allow for responses and discussion.

- Why was David able to defeat Goliath?
- When you face something that scares you or something that requires you to be strong, do you trust in God to help you?
- Do you believe that God can use his strength in you to do great things?
- Do you believe that God will give his strength to those who do not trust in him?

Activity: David's Diary

Materials: *A sheet of writing paper for each child, pens or pencils for each child*

Distribute a piece of paper and a pen or pencil to each child. Ask the children to imagine that they are David about to face Goliath and that they are writing in their diary. Have them write a prayer that David might have prayed to God before facing Goliath. After they complete their prayers, invite volunteers to share their prayers with the group.

Memory Verse Activity: Shepherd's bags

"The Lord is my strength and my shield." (Psalm 28:7a)

Materials: *Brown felt squares, thin leather roping (sold at most craft stores), smooth stones (also sold at craft stores or home supply stores), small slips of paper, pens or pencils*

Before the Session: Your class will use these materials to make shepherd's bags. Before class, punch holes around the edges of the felt squares approximately one inch apart. Cut the roping in lengths long enough to be threaded through the holes and with enough left over to use as a strap to hold the bag. Display the memory verse on a marker board or posterboard.

Give each child a felt square, leather roping, five stones, a slip of paper, and a pen or pencil. Assist the children in threading the roping through the holes of the felt squares. Leave about four inches of roping hanging out of the first and last holes you thread. You can tie these ends together to draw the pouch closed. Place the five stones inside the shepherd's bag. Tell the children that these bags may have been like the shepherd's bag David carried with him when he defeated Goliath. Then have the children write the memory verse on their slip of paper and place it in their bag.

Pray

Remind the children that God's strength is stronger than anything we know on earth.

Pray together, thanking God for the strength God gives. Ask God to help us learn to trust that God's strength will go with us when we face difficulties and fears.

Session 3

WHEN I AM AFRAID, I DEPEND ON MY FRIENDS

1 SAMUEL 20

Teacher's Introduction

This session emphasizes the value of friendship. In 1 Samuel 20, we find the story of Jonathan and David. As you study their story with your class, guide the children to understand that they can depend on friends in times of trouble. Help them learn that it is important for them to be a good friend to others with difficulties in their lives.

Introductory Activity: Sticking Together

Materials: 20 balloons, two large plastic garbage bags

Before the Session: Blow up the balloons. Place ten inflated balloons in each garbage bag.

Place the class into two teams. Each team should then choose one person to be "It." The rest of the team should stand in a circle around the person who is "It." The object of the game is for the team to cover their person with the balloons. Explain that each team should rub the balloons on their heads to create static on the balloons. Then they should stick the balloons to the person who is "It." The teams will compete to see who can get their ten balloons to stick first. Give the start signal and begin.

When the game ends, remind your class that this game was a fun way to remind us that friends stick together in good times and in bad times (like the balloons stuck to their teammates). Ask the children to share times when a friend has stuck with them in a difficult situation.

Introduction of 1 Samuel 20

Talk with the children about today's session: "When I Am Afraid, I Depend on My Friends." Tell them that they will learn more about David, the boy who defeated Goliath. David had a good friend named Jonathan, and the two of them stuck together during a very difficult situation. Encourage the children to think about the importance of being faithful and helpful to our friends.

Biblical Lesson: 1 Samuel 20

Materials: Large pieces of construction paper or posterboard, marker, tape

Before the Session: Write the sequence of events from the Bible lesson (see below) on the construction paper or posterboard. Prior to the activity, spread the strips on a table or floor where the children can read them. They should not be in sequential order.

Have the children work together to put the events in sequential order before you tell them the story. After they hear today's story, they will return to the sequence they chose and make any corrections necessary.

Sequence of Events
Write one event per piece of paper, or four events per large piece of posterboard (cut the posterboard into sentence strips). Be sure to omit the number before each statement.

1. King Saul wants to kill David.
2. David asks Jonathan why King Saul wants to kill him.
3. David and Jonathan come up with a plan and make an oath of friendship to each other.
4. David hides in the field.
5. King Saul asks Jonathan where David has gone.
6. Jonathan questions King Saul about why he wants to kill David, and King Saul becomes very angry with Jonathan.
7. Jonathan shoots arrows to warn David to flee.
8. Jonathan and David have a tearful goodbye.

Use the following paraphrase as a guide to tell your class the story of Jonathan and David's friendship. Another option is to use a Bible storybook or tell the story in your own words, being sure to include the events listed above or to modify the events to correspond with the version you tell.

Jonathan and David

After David's mighty triumph over Goliath, he became a part of Saul's army. Saul was jealous of David because he did everything so well, and the people praised David for all his good acts. This angered King Saul so much that he wanted to kill David.

While David was a part of Saul's army, he and Saul's son Jonathan became best friends. They loved each other very much and stuck with each other even through difficult times.

David went to Jonathan and asked him, "What have I done? What is my crime? Why does your father want to kill me?" Jonathan didn't know why his father wanted to kill David, but David took an oath and said, "Your father knows very well that we are friends. He would not tell you if he wanted to kill me." Jonathan believed David and told him, "Whatever you want me to do, I'll do for you."

So David and Jonathan came up with a plan. The next day David was supposed to dine with King Saul at a festival meal, but instead of going to the meal he would go and hide in the field. David told Jonathan, "If your father misses me, tell him I had to go to Bethlehem. If he says, 'very well,' then you will know that I am safe. But if he loses his temper, you will know that he wants to harm me."

Jonathan the Brave
(Illustration Credit: Barclay Burns)

Jonathan told David that he would make a signal so that David would know if the king was still angry with him. He would shoot three arrows to the side of the stone where David was hiding. Jonathan said to David, "I will send a boy and say, 'Go, find the arrows.' If I say to him, 'Look, the arrows are on this side of you; bring them here,' then come out of your hiding place. That will be the signal that Saul is not planning to harm you. But if I say to the boy, 'Look, the arrows are beyond you,' then you must go, because Saul is angry and wants to kill you."

So David hid in the field, and Jonathan went to the festival meal. King Saul asked Jonathan where David was. When Jonathan told him, Saul became very angry. Jonathan asked Saul, "Why do you want to kill David? What has he done?" Saul became even angrier and hurled his spear at Jonathan. Then Jonathan knew that his father wanted to kill David.

Jonathan got up from the table and left the festival meal. The next morning he went out to the field and shot his arrows to warn David that Saul was trying to kill him. When David understood the message, he got up from behind the stone and bowed down before Jonathan three times. Then they kissed each other and cried together.

Jonathan said to David, "Go in peace, for we have sworn friendship with each other in the name of the Lord." Then David left, and Jonathan went back to the town.

Review Activity: After you have told the story to your class, return to the sequence of events that they put in order before they heard the story. Help them make any corrections and review the story as you work together to put the events in the right order.

Then ask the following or similar questions to your class for review and discussion.

- How could you tell that Jonathan and David were good friends?
- Could David depend on Jonathan to help him when he was afraid?
- Do you have good friends who will help you when you are afraid?
- Are you helpful to your friends when they are afraid?

Activity: Friendship Bracelets

Materials: Craft string used with beads (available at most craft stores), beads of various colors (available at most craft stores), scissors

Before the Session: Cut the lengths of string long enough to make bracelets. Leave extra string to tie off each end of the bracelet. Provide enough supplies for each child to make two bracelets. Set the beads and strings on a table where the children will work.

Tell the children that they are going to make friendship bracelets. One of the bracelets will be for them to keep. The other bracelet will be for them to give to a special friend—someone that they know will always help them when they need a friend. Have the children tie one end of their string so that the beads will not slip off as they make their bracelets. Then they can begin threading beads onto their string. When they have reached the desired length, tie off the opposite end and then tie the two ends together.

Memory Verse Activity

"There is a friend who sticks closer than a brother." (Proverbs 18:24b)

Materials: Drawing paper, crayons or markers, pencils or pens

Before the Session: Set out supplies and write the memory verse on a marker board or sheet of posterboard.

Ask the children to use the art supplies to draw a picture of themselves and one of their close friends. At the top or bottom of the page, have them write the memory verse. When the children have completed their pictures, ask volunteers to tell the class about their friend and why they consider that person a good friend.

Pray

Remind the children that God gives us friends who will be there for us when we need them. God also wants us to be good friends to others.

Pray together, thanking God for friends. Ask God to help us be good and faithful friends.

Session 4

WHEN I AM AFRAID, I REMEMBER GOD'S PROMISES

2 SAMUEL 7:1-17

Teacher's Introduction

In 2 Samuel 7:1-17, we read about God's promises to David. God reminds David that he brought him from the pasture to the palace and that he has delivered him from his enemies. Now he promises David that he will make his name great and give the people of Israel a home.

The promises God made to David remind us of the promises that are also ours. This lesson guides your children to remember that God's promises are also for his children today, and that they can trust in God's promises in times of fear and uncertainty.

Introductory Activity: From Pasture to Palace

Materials: *Two long strips of butcher paper or bulletin board paper; markers and crayons; pencils; nature items such as twigs, small branches, leaves, etc.; cotton balls; glue; scrap fabric; tape*

Before the Session: For this activity you will place your class into two groups. One group will create a pasture scene on one of the long strips of paper. They can use markers and crayons to draw the pasture, then glue on the nature items to enhance their pasture scene. They can use the cotton balls to make sheep in the pasture. The second group will create a palace scene. They can use markers and crayons to draw their scene, then use the fabric scraps to create flags or banners for the palace. They can also use the nature items to create bushes and trees around the palace. Place the items needed for each group in the area where you want them to work.

Place the class into two groups, giving them their assignments and the materials they will need. Encourage them to work together to create their scenes. When each scene is completed, tape them on opposite walls of the classroom.

Introduction of 2 Samuel 7:1-17

Talk with the children about today's session: "When I Am Afraid, I Remember God's Promises." Tell them that today's story is once again about David, the boy who defeated Goliath, became a part of Saul's army, and had a great friendship with Jonathan. Discuss the pictures the children made in the introductory activity, telling them that David is now a great king—he went from the pasture to the palace. Today we will learn about the promises God made to the good king, David.

Biblical Lesson: 2 Samuel 7:1-17

Materials: Construction paper, scissors, marker

Before the Session: Write the promises of God to David (listed below) on pieces of construction paper and cut them apart. (The verse numbers are for your own reference.)

Distribute the prepared promises to the children in your class. Have those children read the promises at the places indicated in the lesson as you tell the story.

Promise 1: I will make your name great, like the names of the greatest men of the earth. (v. 9)
Promise 2: I will provide a place for my people Israel. (v. 10)
Promise 3: I will also give you rest from all your enemies. (v. 11)
Promise 4: The Lord will establish a house for you. (v. 11)
Promise 5: I will raise up your children to succeed you. (v. 12)
Promise 6: I will establish a kingdom through your children. (v. 12)
Promise 7: My love will never be taken away from him. (v. 15)
Promise 8: Your house and your kingdom will endure forever before me; your throne will be established forever. (v. 16)

God's Promises to David

After King David was settled in his palace and the LORD had given him rest from all his enemies around him, he said to Nathan the prophet, "Here I am, living in a palace of cedar, while the ark of God remains in a tent."

Nathan replied to the king, "Whatever you have in mind, go ahead and do it, for the LORD is with you."

That night the word of the LORD came to Nathan, saying: "Go and tell my servant David, 'This is what the LORD says: I took you from the pasture and from following the flock to be ruler over my people Israel. I have been with you wherever you have gone, and I have cut off all your enemies from before you. Now, **(read Promise #1)**. And **(read Promise #2)**. I will plant the people so that they can have a home of their own and no longer be disturbed. Wicked people will not harm them anymore. **(Read Promise #3)**.

The LORD declares to you that **(read Promise #4)**. When your days are over and you rest with your fathers, **(read Promise #5)**, and **(read Promise #6)**. Your son will be the one who will build a house for my Name, and I will establish the throne of his kingdom forever. I will be his father, and he will be my son. When he does wrong, I will punish him. But **(read Promise #7)**. **(Read Promise #8)**."

Review Questions: Ask the following or similar questions to your class for review and discussion. Allow for responses after each question.

- Do you believe that God could do all of the things he promised David he would do?
- How do you think God's promises made David feel?
- Does God keep his promises?
- Have you ever made a promise to someone? Did you keep your promise?
- How does it feel when a promise is broken?
- Does God make promises to us today?
- Do you believe that God will keep his promises today?

Activity: Promise Pillowcases

Materials: *White pillowcases, fabric paints and/or fabric pens*

Before the Session: Lay the pillowcases out flat on a table. Place a piece of cardboard or posterboard inside the pillowcase to absorb the paint that bleeds through. Place fabric paints in the area where you will be working. Write Psalm 145:13b on a marker board or posterboard and display it where the children can see it. ("The LORD is faithful to all his promises.")

Explain to the children that they will make "Promise Pillowcases." These pillowcases will remind them that God will be faithful to keep his promises. Have the children write the words "The LORD is faithful to all his promises" on their pillowcases using the fabric pens (assist where needed). Then encourage them to decorate them with the fabric paints.

Memory Verse Activity

"The LORD is faithful to all his promises and loving toward all he has made." (Psalm 145:13b)

Materials: Markers

Before the Session: Display the memory verse where the children can see it.

Talk with the children about how God was faithful to David. God guided David when he was a shepherd in the pasture taking care of sheep. God was with David when he was a great king living in a palace. As we discovered today, God made several promises to David, and God was faithful to keep those promises. David knew that he could count on God when he was afraid.

Give each child a marker, then ask them to go to the pasture scene or the palace scene that they made in the first activity. Have each child write the memory verse somewhere on those scenes.

Pray

Remind the children that God keeps promises. Tell them that God has made promises to them, and when they are afraid, they can remember God's good promises.

Say a prayer together, thanking God for God's promises and God's faithfulness to David and to us.

Session 5

WHEN I AM AFRAID, I WORSHIP GOD

2 SAMUEL 22

Teacher's Introduction

Second Samuel 22 is a song of praise. It is David's song of praise to God for his faithfulness in delivering him from his enemies. This song is a beautiful example of worship. In this last session of the "When I Am Afraid" lessons, your class will study David's song and be reminded that in times of fear and doubt they can turn to God in worship and praise.

Introductory Activity: A Worship Brainstorm

Materials: A piece of butcher paper or bulletin board paper, marker, tape

Before the Session: Draw an outline of a church building on the paper. At the top of the paper write the phrase "Worship Brainstorm." Tape the paper to a wall or bulletin board.

Tell the class that you want them to have a worship brainstorm. Explain what it means to brainstorm—to say whatever ideas come to mind about a certain topic. Then ask the children to think about worship and to say aloud the words that come to mind. Write their responses inside the outline of the church you have drawn.

Some examples of the kind of words they may suggest are hymns, sermons, singing, praying, choir, etc.

When the activity is complete, talk about the words the children chose. Discuss what it means to worship—to adore someone or to admire someone.

In worship we adore God. We tell him how much we love him and appreciate who he is.

Introduction of 2 Samuel 22

Talk with the children about today's session: "When I Am Afraid, I Worship God." Remind them that the stories in 1 and 2 Samuel were written when the Israelites lived in a strange land. Worshiping God was important to them and probably made them feel closer to God in times of fear and loneliness. Tell the children that worship can also make us feel closer to God. Today we will learn about a song of worship and praise that David sang to God. This song can teach us ways to praise and worship God.

Biblical Lesson: 2 Samuel 22

Materials: Pieces of drawing paper for each child, pencils, crayons, small strips of paper

Before the Session: Write the following Bible verses on the strips of paper:
2 Samuel 22:2-4
2 Samuel 22:8-14
2 Samuel 22:17-20
2 Samuel 22:29-30
2 Samuel 22:31-33

Place the children into five groups. Distribute paper, pencils, and crayons. Give each group one of the Bible verses that you have written on the paper strips. Explain to them that these are verses from David's song of praise and worship to God. Remind them that he sang this song to thank God for delivering him from his enemies. Ask them to read the verses together, then individually draw something that represents those verses. For example, 2 Samuel 22:2-4 speak of God as a rock and a fortress. Verses 8-14 speak of the earth trembling and of God parting the heavens and coming down with dark clouds under his feet. Verses 17-20 speak of God as a rescuer. Verses 29-30 speak of God as a lamp, and vv. 31-33 speak of God as a shield.

When they have completed their pictures, have each group read their verses to the entire class and share their drawings.

Tell the children that one way to worship God is through art. The drawings they made today are actually praises to God!

Responsive Reading Based on 2 Samuel 22:47-51

Materials: *Copies of the responsive reading for each child*

Talk with the children about ways they have worshiped God today (coming to church to Bible study, praying, drawing). Another way to worship God is to read the Scriptures. Introduce the responsive reading from 2 Samuel 22:47-51, and encourage the children to read the corresponding parts in praise to God.

Girls: The Lord lives!
Boys: Praise be to my Rock!
Girls: Exalted be God, the Rock, my Savior!
Boys: He is the God who avenges me,
Girls: Who puts the nations under me,
Boys: Who sets me free from my enemies.
Girls: You exalted me above my foes;
Boys: From violent men you rescued me.
Girls: Therefore I will praise you, O Lord, among the nations;
Boys: I will sing praises to your name.
Girls: He gives his king great victories;
Boys: He shows unfailing kindness to his anointed,
Girls: To David and his descendants forever.
All: The Lord lives! Praise be to my Rock!

Review Activity

Ask the following or similar questions to your class for review and discussion. Allow for responses after each question.

- In our Bible lesson today we used art and Scripture reading to worship and praise God. What are some other things that you can do or participate in to worship God? (sing, pray, give an offering, etc.)
- How do you think we should behave in worship?
- Does worship help you feel closer to God?
- Can you only worship God in a church on Sunday morning?

- Where are some other places that we can worship God?

Activity: Worshiping God with Our Own Words

Materials: Writing paper, pencils

Ask children to think about how they feel about God, then give them writing paper and pencils to write words of praise and worship to God. Their writing can be a song, a poem, or just a few sentences. Tell them that these words are private—between them and God.

Memory Verse Activity

"I call to the LORD, who is worthy of praise." (2 Samuel 22:4a)

Materials: Construction paper, markers

Before the Session: Cut the construction paper in half. You will need eleven squares of construction paper. Write one word from the Bible verse and the reference on each square.

Scramble the words of the Bible verse and spread the squares on a table or floor. Have the class to work together to unscramble the verse. Have them recite it together, then ask them to choose one word to be removed. Remove the word, and recite the verse again. Continue in this manner until all the words have been removed and the class can recite the verse from memory.

Pray

Remind the children that there are many ways to worship God. They can go to church, sing, experience nature, draw, write, show love to people, and share with others. Prayer is another way to worship God.

Lead your class to say sentence prayers out loud. Encourage a time of prayerful worship and praise to God.

TEACHING 1 & 2 SAMUEL TO YOUTH

Listen to the Words

Music has been hailed as the universal language of the world. It may also be considered the primary language of youth. This series of lessons guides youth to reflect upon four songs recorded in the Books of 1 and 2 Samuel. They will study these songs and the stories that surround them from the perspective of the Israelite exiles who would have remembered and recorded the songs while in captivity. The youth will discuss why these particular songs were remembered and why they provided hope to those who remembered them. They will also survey the music of their generation and their faith to assess its potential for providing hope.

As you guide your students through biblical texts and numerous musical compositions, encourage them to "listen to the Word" and "listen to the words."

Outline of Sessions and Texts

Session 1: Listen to the Words—An Introduction to the Exilic Experience
   Psalm 137
Session 2: Listen to the Words when You Are Doubting
   1 Samuel 2:1-10
Session 3: Listen to the Words when You Are Weak
   1 Samuel 18:5-9
Session 4: Listen to the Words when You Are Hurting
   2 Samuel 1:17-27
Session 5: Listen to the Words when You Are Reflecting
   2 Samuel 22:2-51

Suggested Supplies

During each learning session, you should have the following items available: a Bible and a hymnal for each student and a CD/cassette player. Encourage the students to bring several of their favorite CDs and/or cassettes to each session. (Bring a few of your own as well. Participate in discussion and sharing of music, but do not dominate.)

SESSION 1
LISTEN TO THE WORDS: AN INTRODUCTION TO THE EXILIC EXPERIENCE

Learning Goal: Help youth understand the contexts in which the events of 1 and 2 Samuel occurred (the united monarchy) and were later remembered (the Babylonian exile).
Focal Text: Psalm 137

Teaching Plan

Use the following steps to guide your learners through the session. Adapt suggested activities and questions to suit your particular group.

(1) As students gather, have Elton John's "Sad Songs Say So Much" playing in the background.
- What does Elton John mean by the title?
- What sad songs do you know?
- Are there "happy songs" that make you sad when you hear them because of memories they invoke?

(2) Instruct the students to read the focal text—Psalm 137.
- What do you think is happening in this text?
- What feelings are being expressed by the Israelites?
- Why did they not want to sing?

(3) Share a brief summary of the history of Israel.
- Use information from chapter 1 of this book.
- Highlight the idea that the stories in 1 and 2 Samuel occurred during the united monarchy, but were remembered and recorded during the Babylonian exile.
- Ask students to imagine what enslavement and exile would be like.
- Conclude with the idea that the songs recorded in 1 and 2 Samuel are primarily "oldies" that were remembered and recorded during the exile.

(4) Encourage the students to discuss the songs of their generation.
- What are your favorite songs?
- How do these songs make you feel?
- What bands, artists, or songs will define your generation?
- What events or people do you connect with particular songs?
- When you are older, how will you feel when you remember these songs, events, and people?

(5) Encourage the students to discuss the "songs of Zion."
- Why were the Babylonians asking the Israelites to sing?
- How would you imaginatively describe the songs of Zion?
- How might the Israelites feel if they sang their songs in a strange land?
- In Psalm 137 the Israelites did not want to sing, but 1 and 2 Samuel contain four songs. What changed their minds?

(6) Guide the students to understand music as a medium of faith and hope.
- Can you think of a song from your generation that might encourage you in a time of crisis?
- Look through the provided hymnal and find a song of faith that might encourage a person in crisis.

(7) Pray together, thanking God for musicians who provide us with melodies and words that help us in times of crisis.

SESSION 2
LISTEN TO THE WORDS WHEN YOU ARE DOUBTING

Learning Goal: Help students understand the importance of professing our faith even when we are struggling with our faith.
Focal Text: 1 Samuel 2:1-10

Teaching Plan

Use the following steps to guide your learners through the session. Adapt suggested activities and questions to suit your particular group.

(1) As students gather, have "I'm a Believer" performed by the Monkees or Smash Mouth playing in the background.
- To what does the song "I'm a Believer" refer?
- Do you ever have a "trace of doubt in your mind" about your love for a certain person or a certain person's love for you?
- Would a trace of doubt keep you from singing the song about someone you love? Why or why not?

(2) Instruct the students to read silently 1 Samuel 1:1-28.
- What pains did Hannah endure because she was barren?
- In what ways did Hannah remain faithful to God?
- How do you imagine she felt about God before having a child? After?

(3) Read Hannah's song in 1 Samuel 2:1-10.
- What affirmations or professions does Hannah make about God?
- Did she believe these things before she had a child?
- Would there have been a "trace of doubt" in her mind?

(4) Ask students to imagine they are exiled Israelites in Babylon.
- How would an exiled slave relate to Hannah's story?
- What doubts would an exile have about God?
- Why would an exiled slave sing Hannah's song?

(5) Guide the students to understand that doubt is healthy, normal, and often addressed in music as well as other elements of worship.

- What do you think about the following statement? "Worship is where we go to say what we believe, even when we are not sure we believe it."
- What are some questions or doubts you have entertained?
- Are there songs from your generation that address the issues of doubt or belief?
- Look through the provided hymnal and find a song that states something you believe.

(6) Pray together, thanking God for worship that provides the opportunity to question, a graceful community in which to question, and mediums of music, litany, prayers, Scriptures, and sermons that affirm our beliefs in the midst of questions.

SESSION 3
LISTEN TO THE WORDS WHEN YOU ARE WEAK

Learning Goal: Help youth understand that size, age, and resources have little to do with real power.
Focal Text: 1 Samuel 18:5-9

Teaching Plan

Use the following steps to guide your learners through the session. Adapt suggested activities and questions to suit your particular group.

(1) Before the session, read the story of David from 1 Samuel 16 to 1 Samuel 24. From this section of David's life, create a competitive game with trivial facts the youth might know from their Sunday school participation. (What giant did David kill? Who was David's best friend? What was David's father's name? Etc.) Be creative with the game's format.

(2) As students enter the room, place them into teams and immediately begin the competition. For added atmosphere, you may have a "Jock Jams" or other similar sports CD playing in the background. (It won't help increase attention but it will enliven the moment.) At the end of the game, announce the winners,

award a cheap prize, and play the song "We Are the Champions" by Queen. (Note: You want the winners to feel like winners and the losers to feel like losers for later discussion.)

(3) Read 1 Samuel 18:5-7 to the youth.
- What do we know of David's youth until this point? (young or old, talents, etc.)
- How did the singing of the women make David feel?

(4) Read 1 Samuel 18:8-9 to the youth.
- What do we know about Saul?
- How did the song make Saul feel?

(5) Discuss the game with which you began the session.
- How many of you knew the song "We Are the Champions"?
- Have you heard it at sporting events? What was the context?
- How did each of you feel during the awards ceremony earlier in the session? Winners? Losers?
- How have people reacted to this song and others like it at sporting events you've attended?
- Have you ever heard "the losers" singing this song and shouting, "We're number one"? Why do they do that?

(6) Discuss the exilic situation.
- Why would the exiled Israelites remember and sing the song in 1 Samuel 18:7?
- To whom would they relate in the song? Why?
- How do you think the song made them feel?

(7) Help the youth connect with the text.
- Do you ever feel too young, too small, or too inadequate to do something special for God?
- What are some of your weaknesses?
- What are some of your spiritual weaknesses?
- How could you improve in these areas of your life?
- What could you do to overcome these weaknesses completely in your life?
- What are some things you can do for God right now?

- If you had to choose a song from your generation to be your "theme song" or just to keep you "pumped up" in the quest to defeat your weaknesses and be useful to God, what would it be? (Play some of their theme songs if they have the CDs.)

(8) Pray together, thanking God that he can use us right now, just as we are.

SESSION 4
LISTEN TO THE WORDS WHEN YOU ARE HURTING

Learning Goal: Help youth discuss and live with loss.
Focal Text: 2 Samuel 1:17-27

Teaching Plan

Use the following steps to guide your learners through the session. Adapt suggested activities and questions to suit your particular group.

(1) As students gather, have the song "Tears in Heaven" by Eric Clapton playing.

(2) Have students reflect upon songs that were written in the event of a death.
- Ask if anyone knows what precipitated Eric Clapton's composition of "Tears in Heaven." (His child fell from an open hotel window and died.)
- Locate and tell the story behind the hymn "It Is Well with My Soul."
- Ask the students to share songs that have been written for or are closely associated with deaths of individuals. Share others of which you are aware.

(3) Instruct the students to read silently 2 Samuel 1:17-27.
- What is a lamentation?
- Describe David's relationship with Saul and Jonathan.
- Why would David lament each of their deaths?
- What feelings does David convey in this song?

(4) Help the students share about their own experiences with loss and death.
- What experiences have you had with death?
- Who is the closest person to you that has died in your lifetime?
- What feelings and thoughts did you experience?
- What other types of losses have you experienced?

(5) Help the students connect with the exiled Israelites.
- Why would the exiled Israelites remember this song?
- What losses do you think they experienced moving into and through a time of exile?
- How would David's lament over Saul and Jonathan benefit the exiled Israelites?

(6) Tell the students that music often helps us express emotions we find difficult to verbalize.
- What songs from your generation address the issue of loss?
- Locate hymns in your hymnal that give hope in loss.

(7) Pray together, thanking God for melodies and lyrics that help us express our deepest pains.

SESSION 5
LISTEN TO THE WORDS WHEN YOU ARE REFLECTING

Learning Goal: Help youth understand that God is present throughout our life journeys; God exists in the highs and lows and everything in between.
Focal Text: 2 Samuel 22

Teaching Plan

Use the following steps to guide your learners through the session. Adapt suggested activities and questions to suit your particular group.

(1) As students gather, ask them to be seated and listen carefully to Cat Stevens's song "Cat's in the Cradle."
- Using your imagination with regard to the characters in this song, tell the father's "life story."
- Tell the son's "life story."

(2) Ask the students to think about the music of their generation.
- What songs of their generation tell a story?
- How are songs used in musicals (theater, cinema, etc.) to move story lines along?
- What musicals have you seen and what songs were memorable?
- How did these memorable songs function in the story?
- Is there a particular song that summarizes or symbolizes the story of your life? What is it?

(3) Ask the students to read silently 2 Samuel 22.
- How does David poetically describe some of the best times of his life?
- How does he describe some of the worst times?
- What are specific incidents to which he may be referring?
- How does David describe God's presence during these incidents?
- Do you think he felt the same way when he actually experienced the incidents, or are these words more reflective?

(4) Broaden the students' knowledge of David by sharing a brief summary of the major incidents in his life. Use the outline provided in the "Guiding the Learner" section of chapter 4.

(5) Ask the students to share their life stories.
- What have been some of your best times?
- What have been some of your worst times?
- Has God seemed present or absent during these times?
- How have you recognized or sought for God during these times?

(6) End this session and the series by helping youth connect with the exiled Israelite community.
- What were some of the best times in Israel's history?
- What were some of the worst?

- Why would this final song of David be so important for the exiled Israelites to remember?

(7) Instruct the youth to search the hymnal for songs that affirm God's presence and care in our lives. Either read or sing a few of the hymns together.

(8) Pray together, thanking God for being present in every chapter of our lives.

www.ingramcontent.com/pod-product-compliance
Lightning Source LLC
LaVergne TN
LVHW051558080426
835510LV00020B/3035